awa
399
2/22/16

The Fall of Camelot

A Study of Tennyson's "Idylls of the King"

John D. Rosenberg

The Belknap Press of Harvard University Press, Cambridge, Massachusetts 1973

211434

To M. J. R.
1924–1944

"Frater Ave atque Vale"

Acknowledgments

In the course of writing this book I have incurred many debts of gratitude that I am pleased to acknowledge. Much of the manuscript was drafted in 1969, when, as a Guggenheim Fellow and Visiting Fellow at Clare Hall, I was resident in Cambridge, England. The sudden transition from time-poor New York to time-rich Cambridge served to crystallize my ideas about mutability in Tennyson's poetry, particularly in the *Idylls of the King*. In writing about Tennyson's great elegy to the fall of the West, I found myself influenced by this ancient center where the young Tennyson formed his deepest friendships and where much that is still vital in our culture splendidly survives. All his life Tennyson was haunted by that part of his past he shared with Arthur Hallam at Cambridge. In *In Memoriam* he recalls his anguished return to Hallam's vacant rooms at Trinity College, and he spent over half a century memorializing Hallam in his two "Arthuriads"—*In Memoriam* and *Idylls of the King*. The Library of Trinity College contains manuscripts of these and other poems of Tennyson's, and I am indebted to the present Lord Tennyson, the Tennyson Trustees, and the Master and Fellows of Trinity College for permission to quote from these unpublished sources. I am also indebted to the Colbeck Collection at the University of British Columbia for placing its rare Tennyson materials at my disposal.

Professor Jerome H. Buckley first opened my eyes to the *Idylls* almost two decades ago in his Victorian seminar at

Columbia University; I believe he will forgive me if some of his own astute perceptions have found their unacknowledged way into this book. In the decade since I have been directing the same seminar at Columbia, my own insights have come back to me, transformed and enriched, in the essays of my students. Here I must especially thank J. Philip Eggers, Barbara Friedberg, Pearl Chesler, Elizabeth Helsinger, George Leonard, and all my other students with whom I have jointly explored the "many-corridored complexities" of Camelot. My friend James Merriman generously let me see his own manuscript on the *Idylls* before I began my own. To Drs. Elinor Shaffer and Barbara Rosenberg I am indebted beyond the mere conventions of acknowledgment for their critical reading of the book in its earlier stages. My colleague Louis Cornell subjected the finished manuscript to the keenest scrutiny, for which I am most grateful. Finally, I should like to thank my wife, Maurine, and Charles Wendel, my research assistant, for their vital assistance in preparing the manuscript for publication.

New York   J. D. R.
February 1973

Contents

Note on Citations

Notes that contribute substantively to the text are indicated by asterisks and appear at the bottom of the page. Notes that simply document a point are indicated by numerical superscripts and are gathered at the end of the book. Poetry citations are to line number unless otherwise specified. Citations from the *Idylls of the King* are given in parentheses immediately after the quotation and are abbreviated as follows:

"The Coming of Arthur"	CA
"Gareth and Lynette"	GL
"The Marriage of Geraint"	MG
"Geraint and Enid"	GE
"Balin and Balan"	BB
"Merlin and Vivien"	MV
"Lancelot and Elaine"	LE
"The Holy Grail"	HG
"Pelleas and Ettarre"	PE
"The Last Tournament"	LT
"Guinevere"	G
"The Passing of Arthur"	PA

*Poetry is like shot-silk with many glancing colours.
Every reader must find his own interpretation according
to his ability, and according to his sympathy with the poet.*
                                                —*Tennyson*

1 · Dispelling the Mists

The *Idylls of the King* is one of the four or five
indisputably great long poems in our language. Yet
Tennyson's doom-laden prophecy of the fall of the West has
been dismissed as a Victorian-Gothic fairy tale. So colossal
a misreading bears witness to the power of the critical
orthodoxy that for the past fifty years has obscured our
perception of the Victorian poets in general and of Tennyson
in particular.

The brilliantly biased essays of T. S. Eliot and the
once-salutory fervors of F. R. Leavis in *New Bearings in
English Poetry* (1932) have created a mythic literary country
in which all of Victorian poetry figures as a Waste Land and
the reader is rushed directly from Keats to Yeats to Eliot,
with no stops on the way save for Gerard Manley Hopkins,
who, Leavis contends, bears "no relation . . . to any
nineteenth-century poet."[1] Since Hopkins is clearly a fine
poet, so the argument assumes, he cannot have been a
Victorian and, by some chronological sleight of hand, he is
translated whole into the twentieth century. The fault with
this mythic map is that it bypasses one of the major English
poets. Yet so great was the need of the first half of the
twentieth century to free itself from the all-dominating voice
of the greatest poet of the nineteenth century that the act
of omission was achieved virtually without protest.

One consequence of this distorted literary map is that
Hopkins has figured as a kind of atemporal freak of the
Muses utterly divorced from his own culture. Hence we have
monographs on Hopkins the Modern, the Jesuit, the Scotist,
but very little indeed on Hopkins the Victorian, the
contemporary of Tennyson, the admirer of Ruskin and
student of Pater, the late-born child of the Oxford Movement
who, after experiencing a characteristically Victorian crisis
of faith, was received into the Catholic Church by Newman,
himself a self-exiled product of the Oxford which so
profoundly shaped them both. Misled by similar distortions
of literary history and by Eliot's own disingenuous clues,
students of Eliot have traced the formative influence upon
his poetry to the French Symbolists or the English
Metaphysicals but ignored his obvious and overriding
indebtedness to Tennyson, who was a symbolist a half-
century before the Symbolist Movement achieved celebrity.

The attempt to sever Yeats from his nineteenth-century
heritage has proven more difficult, if only because Yeats
repeatedly acknowledged its influence upon him. His early
indebtedness to Keats, Tennyson, Morris, Rossetti, and the
Aesthetes is beyond dispute. Of course Yeats's greatness
lies in his transcendence of his Pre-Raphaelite sources, in
the "terrible beauty" that he later created out of the lesser
beauties of lake isles and shadowy waters. Yet like Tennyson
himself, whom he called "the supreme artist,"[2] Yeats built
upon rather than abandoned his early aestheticism. Just as
Tennyson in time transformed the proto-decadent "Palace
of Art" into the Sacred Mount of Camelot, so Yeats
transformed his Pre-Raphaelite borrowings into the eternal
artifice of Byzantium. Both Camelot and Byzantium are holy
cities of the imagination, and Yeats's visionary kingdom
closely borders on Tennyson's Camelot. It is not in
Byzantium but in the *Idylls of the King* that a courtier has
a "Yeatsian" vision of bright birds in gilded cages and
dreams that

lords and ladies of the high court went
In silver tissue talking things of state.

(MG, 662–663)

The road leading back to Camelot passes through
Byzantium and Eliot's *The Waste Land*. But the path will
not be found until the bias of the modernist myth is broken.
English poetry, so the orthodoxy holds, reached a dead-end
with the Victorians. If it is to revive at all, it must develop,
in Leavis' words, "along some other line than that running
from the Romantics through Tennyson, Swinburne, *A
Shropshire Lad*, and Rupert Brooke."[3] Such a line, of course,
never existed; Leavis has yoked the living to the dead and
practices a kind of guilt by moribund association. He did
not see, and Eliot as a practicing poet could not afford to see,
that the great divide in English poetry occurred in 1798,
with the publication of the *Lyrical Ballads*, and not between
the death of Tennyson in 1892 and the appearance of *The
Waste Land* in 1922. The ghost of Tennyson breathes
everywhere in Eliot's verse. But until that ghost is seen
full-face, Tennyson will remain virtually inaccessible to
contemporary readers, "a Virgil among the Shades," as Eliot
felicitously calls him, Eliot himself having consigned
Tennyson to limbo.[4] But it is the nature of ghosts to haunt
us, and now that Eliot, too, is "among the Great in Limbo,"
can we any longer distinguish which of their two voices
speaks to us in the following lines?[5]

Why are we weighed upon with heaviness,
And utterly consumed with sharp distress,
While all things else have rest from weariness?
All things have rest: why should we toil alone . . .
Let us alone. What pleasure can we have
To war with evil? Is there any peace
In ever climbing up the climbing wave?
All things have rest, and ripen toward the grave
In silence; ripen, fall and cease . . .

("The Lotos-Eaters")

Where is there an end of it, the soundless wailing,
The silent withering of autumn flowers
Dropping their petals and remaining motionless;
Where is there an end to the drifting wreckage . . .
There is no end of it, the voiceless wailing,
No end to the withering of withered flowers,
To the movement of pain that is painless and motionless,
To the drift of the sea and the drifting wreckage* . . .
                                    (Four Quartets, "The Dry Salvages")

* The following parallels are no less striking:

. . . I wither slowly in thine arms,
Here at the quiet limit of the world,
A white-haired shadow roaming like a dream . . .
How can my nature longer mix with thine?

I have lost my passion: why should I need to keep it
Since what is kept must be adulterated?
I have lost my sight, smell, hearing, taste and touch:
How should I use them for your closer contact?

The first excerpt is from "Tithonus," the second from "Gerontion,"
dramatic monologues by two young poets about the spiritual drought
of old men in a dry season. Wearing the "mask of age," Tennyson
uses the myth of Tithonus—immeasurably old but wedded to
the ever-rejuvenating Dawn—and projects upon it his own suicidal
grief over the death of Arthur Hallam. "Ulysses" and the "Morte
d'Arthur" (the germ of *Idylls of the King*) were drafted in the same
year as "Tithonus," inspired by the same shock of grief, and
embody the same projective use of myth. In "Gerontion" and
The Waste Land Eliot is strikingly Tennysonian not only in cadence
and imagery but also in reanimating myth as a vehicle for structuring
the sense of private alienation and of cultural disintegration. The
point is not that Eliot is a lesser poet for drawing on Tennyson,
or that Tennyson is important to us merely because Eliot echoed him
so persistently, but that Tennyson is remarkably modern in the uses he
makes of myth, uses perhaps as important to Yeats's development
as they were to Eliot's.

(Excerpts from the poetry of T. S. Eliot are reprinted by permission
of Faber and Faber, Ltd., and Harcourt Brace Jovanovich, Inc.,
and are from *Collected Poems 1909–1962* by T. S. Eliot, copyright
1936 by Harcourt Brace Jovanovich; copyright 1963, 1964 by T. S.
Eliot.)

Eliot's essay on *In Memoriam* (1936) marks the pivotal moment when Tennyson might have reemerged as an important voice in English poetry, only to be silenced by Eliot's damning final paragraphs. Eliot handsomely acknowledges Tennyson's claim to greatness in the opening paragraphs and then proceeds to demolish those claims as he discusses the later phase of Tennyson's career. Although Tennyson is perhaps the most extraordinary example of an English poet of major powers who not only maintained but extended those powers to the verge of old age, he withers and fades under Eliot's hand: "Tennyson seems to have reached the end of his spiritual development with *In Memoriam;* there followed no reconciliation, no resolution." Yet it was precisely in the decades following *In Memoriam* (1850) that Tennyson composed the culminating achievement of his career, the *Idylls of the King,* which Eliot dismisses with the glancing sneer, "Tennyson could not tell a story at all."[6]

At the end of the *In Memoriam* essay we find in its most persuasive form the modern myth of "the two Tennysons," a myth not inspired by Tennyson himself, who was remarkably of a piece from birth to death, but necessitated by the dilemma of those gifted critics faced with the evident fact of Tennyson's greatness and their equally evident inhibition of reponse to that greatness. "The surface of Tennyson," Eliot writes, "stirred about with his time. . . . Among the Great in Limbo, [he is] the most instinctive rebel against the society in which he was the most perfect conformist . . . Tennyson faced neither the darkness nor the light, in his later years. The genius, the technical power, persisted to the end, but the spirit had surrendered . . . having turned aside from the journey through the dark night, to become the surface flatterer of his own time."[7] Yet the *Idylls of the King* is precisely such a journey through the dark night, ending on the uninhabited verge of the world, where Arthur's kingdom meets its apocalyptic doom in the "last, dim, weird battle of the west" (PA, 94), a line which Tennyson eerily glossed as "a presentment of human death."[8]

Although modern literature offers no more chilling prospect than the closing books of the *Idylls*, some of the finest minds of the past generation have rejected the poem as mawkishly insincere. Blindness from such sources can itself cast light, as in the case of Harold Nicolson's attempt to cope with the *Idylls* in 1923, an effort less disingenuous than Eliot's a decade later. Nicolson admits to a strong personal admiration for the poem but reserves final judgment on the grounds that, despite the "magnificent poetry," its effect can only "be one of estrangement and hostility, since it is impossible for us to conquer the impression (doubtless an incorrect and transitory impression) that these poems . . . are for the most part intellectually insincere." And he goes on to suggest that, in view of "the peculiar adjustment to which our nervous system has attained in this year 1923," the *Idylls* be the first of Tennyson's works dropped from any collection seeking to interest the modern reader.[9]

Nicolson's truncated edition of Tennyson makes perfect sense for the nervous system of 1923 once one recognizes that the system was in a state of shock from the First World War—a catastrophe of which the *Idylls* is in the profoundest sense a prophecy—and that the seemingly rock-solid values of the Victorians had proved as ephemeral as Camelot itself. Of all the Victorians Tennyson had the best credentials, and was therefore now the most suspect; of all his poems the *Idylls* had been most extravagantly praised, and therefore now must be "intellectually insincere." Neither Nicolson nor Eliot need ever really have read the *Idylls* in order to reject it. The poem was in their culture's bones, and came to them wrapped in precisely the kind of repugnant piety and platitude that made its rejection a mark of one's coming of age. How in 1923 or 1936 could one read a work which, in the words of Tennyson's official biographer and commentator, his son Hallam, "carefully shadowed forth the spiritual progress and advance of the world"?[10]

The Smiling Public Laureate, then, inevitably presented a repugnant face to his post–World War I readers, but there remained the vexing reality of his poetry, and to account for its intermittent power Nicolson invented the brilliant fiction of Tennyson the Poet in Spite of Himself. Nicolson's Tennyson, at heart "a morbid and unhappy mystic," abandoned the true inspiration of his melancholy muse and, allying his shallow intelligence with the values of his time, was forced into fifty years of unnatural objectivity.[11] This image has been reproduced with minor variations by virtually every critic of Tennyson since Nicolson—most notably by Eliot.*

The problem of the two Tennysons is not altogether solved even after we recognize that the critics have projected their own divided sensibility upon the poet. Tennyson himself is deeply at fault, and that fault is one of the chief glories of his poetry. Almost all of his poems that compel our attention today embody an intensely ambiguous conflict of warring elements: of faith versus doubt in *In Memoriam*, of social involvement versus aesthetic withdrawal in "The Lady of Shalott." Many of his best lyrics form pendants to

* W. H. Auden's variant—"He had the finest ear, perhaps, of any English poet; he was also undoubtedly the stupidest"—is so richly absurd that I have in time grown fond of it (W. H. Auden, ed., *A Selection from the Poems of Alfred, Lord Tennyson* [Garden City, N.Y., Doubleday, 1944], p. x). Cf. Cleanth Brooks's fine analysis of "Tears, Idle Tears" in *The Well-Wrought Urn*: in order to account for intellectual subtlety in the work of a Victorian poet, Brooks concludes that Tennyson has *blundered* into ambiguity. The debate over Tennyson's intelligence goes back to his contemporaries and ranges from Arnold's condemnation of him as "deficient in intellectual power" (F. L. Lucas, *Ten Victorian Poets* [Cambridge, Cambridge University Press, 1940], p. 11) to T. H. Huxley's praise of him as one of "the thought-worn chieftains of the mind," the only poet since Lucretius "who has taken the trouble to understand the work and tendency of the men of science" (Jerome H. Buckley, *The Victorian Temper* [Cambridge, Mass., Harvard University Press, 1951], pp. 67, 255). For a useful summary of recent variations on the theme of the two Tennysons, see James D. Kissane, *Alfred Tennyson* (New York, Twayne Publishers, 1970), p. 27.

others, the same theme achieving a contrary resolution in
its companion: the will to act in "Ulysses" versus the
voluptuousness of drugged inaction in "The Lotos-Eaters."
Even within a poem that is seemingly most assertive of a
single point of view, the assertion may prove illusory, as in
"Ulysses," which can be read as a ringing affirmation of life
in the face of adversity and age or, with due stress on the
heavy blank-verse lines, as a withdrawal from family, from
society, from kingship, and ultimately from life, a suicidal
sailing beyond the sunset to join the ghost of the great
Achilles.

The majority of Tennyson's contemporaries were impelled
to find in his poetry morally uplifting solutions, whereas
Tennyson in fact posed morally excruciating dilemmas. His
successors between the two world wars, believing that a
Victorian poet *must* have proffered solutions but finding his
poetry illicitly compelling, concluded that Tennyson was
two-faced. To us who can now trace in Tennyson and the
greatest of his contemporaries the same "journey through the
dark night" that shadows our own lives, the hypothesis of
duplicity blocks our entry into his poetry, just as it once
made possible a partial appreciation for Nicolson and Eliot.

The shift in our capacity to perceive what Tennyson
actually wrote has already occurred in the case of *In
Memoriam*; it has yet to occur with the *Idylls*. Again, Eliot
is the pivotal figure. With a single sentence he brought
In Memoriam into the twentieth century, making Tennyson's
agonized uncertainty relevant to our own: "It is not religious
because of the quality of its faith, but because of the quality
of its doubt." [12] Because Tennyson's contemporaries had
read the poem as a religious affirmation, because Queen
Victoria found in it comfort second only to the Bible, we
could not read it—until the Queen had been proven a dupe.
Yet *In Memoriam* is not about the triumph of doubt over
faith or faith over doubt, but about the tensions and peculiar
affinities between the two. The complex of attitudes

represented by the two words has shifted, and by "faith" the Queen included certain shades of meaning we dignify by the word "doubt," and by "doubt" and "despair" and "dark night" we include certain of the religious attitudes the Queen dignified by "faith." It is Tennyson's unique genius that he could speak both to the believing Queen and to the skeptical present.

That Tennyson's elegy should have been acknowledged a great poem while the *Idylls* has been dismissed is at first glance something of a mystery, for the vision of life the *Idylls* holds up is far closer to our own temper than that of *In Memoriam*. *In Memoriam* begins in death and ends with a marriage feast; the *Idylls* opens with marriage and ends with a funeral. The Arthur of the elegy moves from darkness to "the light of boundless day"; the Arthur of the *Idylls* moves through the light of his coming to the mists of his passing, a setting far truer to Tennyson's infinitely sad, Virgilian sense of the tears and tragic transience inherent in things. It is true, of course, that each poem contains its own counter-movement: the forward progress of *In Memoriam* frequently turns back upon itself, and over the blackness of Arthur's death there breaks the faint light of the winter dawn. But the balance has clearly tipped, and the inversely related patterns of the two poems strongly suggest that Tennyson intended the *Idylls* to be the gloomy sequel to its too sanguine predecessor. "It's too hopeful," Tennyson remarked of *In Memoriam*, "more than I am myself. I think of adding another to it, a speculative one . . . showing that all the arguments are about as good on one side as the other." [13]

Despite its relative optimism, however, *In Memoriam* is much more accessible to us than the *Idylls of the King*. One of the great love poems in English, it speaks to us directly in the confessional voice of the aggrieved poet about the commonest of themes in the simplest of stanzaic forms. The modern reader can feel that here at least Tennyson is himself, not the flattering spokesman of Progress and of the Prince

Consort. The *Idylls of the King*, on the other hand, appears
to be "fancy" Tennyson, an escape from himself and from
the real issues of his own time and ours. One is reminded of
George Meredith's angry comment that Tennyson was
merely "fluting" about unreal figures in an unreal world, and
of his still angrier question, "Isn't there a scent of damned
hypocrisy in all this lisping and vowelled purity of the
Idylls?"[14] So rooted is this suspicion that it has debarred
both the poem's detractors and its admirers from perceiving
an extraordinary fact that thrusts the whole problem of
escapism back upon the reader: The *Idylls of the King* is not
only explicitly and constantly *about* the hazards of mistaking
illusion for reality; it *dramatically enacts* those dangers,
ensnaring the reader in the same delusions that maim and
destroy its characters. Nothing in the poem is as it seems, and
nothing seems to be what it is, with the possible exception
of Arthur, who may himself be the most dangerous of
illusions, the *homme fatal* of the *Idylls*. One passes through
hundreds of lines of some of the most beautiful blank verse in
English, green glades and shimmering towers, knights and
maidens displayed in a rainbow pageant of music and color;
yet the verse, fair as it is, at once unfolds and conceals a
world of the rankest treacheries and vilest horrors: brothers
murder one another, sadistic ladies drive their obsessed
lovers impotent and insane, the King himself is a cuckold,
and the faces of his traitor-knights are ground into
featureless slime. The verse lulls and seduces at the same
time that the events appall; grotesque sights entwine
themselves upon a backround of excruciating clarity and
beauty. Swinburne achieved something of this effect on a
much reduced scale in "The Leper," where he uses an archly
naive diction and rhythm to tell the tale of a necrophiliac
who makes love to the remnants of his lady. But like much
of Swinburne's best verse, "The Leper" makes its own
self-enclosed commentary, emptied of all meaning save the
perfectly poised intensities of sweetness and foulness, beauty

and putridity. A more substantial analogue to Tennyson's
strategy of deceit is Milton's portrait of Satan in *Paradise
Lost*. Satan does not, as Blake believed, get out of Milton's
controlling hand and become his unconscious hero, but is
intended to attract our fallen natures, until we see with a
shock of recognition our own fall mirrored in our sympathy
for the fallen Archangel. In exactly the same way Tennyson
forces his reader to a dramatic recognition that he has
mistaken fair for foul, foul for fair, indeed that it is the
human condition inevitably so to err, and perhaps most to err
when most seeking to avoid such error. Holding a mirror up
to itself, the poem is nowhere what it seems to be—a
medieval charade—but rather the subtlest anatomy of the
failure of ideality in our literature.

Yet the prejudice persists that simply because the *Idylls*
is set in the past it must be dishonestly evasive. This attitude
has a certain plausible modernity but in fact is solidly
Victorian. A sizable body of Tennyson's early critics argued
that the modern poet's business was to portray modern life.
On the most vulgar level, Tennyson was urged not to write
about knights in armor but to compose an epic on Work
or Sanitation. At best the case was put by Ruskin in a letter
to Tennyson occasioned by the publication of the first four
Idylls in 1859. Ruskin himself was in the throes of setting
aside his study of art for his radical critique of English society
and the autobiographical bias of his remarks is apparent,
though nonetheless persuasive:

I am not sure but I feel the art and finish in these poems a
little more than I like to feel it . . . As a description of various
nobleness and tenderness the book is without price: but I
shall always wish it had been nobleness independent of a
romantic condition of externals . . . So great power ought
not to be spent on visions of things past but on the living
present . . . The intense masterful and unerring transcript of
an actuality . . . seems to me the true task of the modern
poet.[15]

Ruskin is surely right in requiring of the modern poet—of
any poet—the intense transcription of an actuality; he is
as surely wrong in assuming that such a transcription can be
made only from the materials of contemporary life. The
dreams of Goya are more real than the hard pictorial surfaces
of Andrew Wyeth, and the odds are that the painter of an
automobile junkyard is more of an escapist, because less of
an artist, than Blake painting the mythical Urizen. For
"escapism" and "realism" in their profoundest meanings are
not functions of time or place but of intensity of imaginative
vision. No prima facie case can be made against the
remoteness of King Arthur that cannot also be made against
his colleague and neighbor, King Lear. Shakespeare turned
from the Elizabethan marketplace to the blasted heaths of
ancient Britain, and in so doing created a Waste Land at
least as contemporary as T. S. Eliot's, or as Tennyson's
blighted land of sand and thorns in "The Holy Grail," from
which Eliot's in part derives. Homer wrote of a war "far on
the ringing plains of windy Troy" that had ended centuries
before his own time, and the Greek tragedians reached into an
even more mythical past in order to create a drama whose
modernity has endured for twenty-five hundred years.

Ironically, the only parts of the *Idylls* which are addressed
to the contemporary moment—the "Dedication" to "Albert
the Good" and the epilogue "To the Queen"—strike us as
irredeemably dated. Yet the great lines in "The Coming of
Arthur" which immediately follow the "Dedication," and
which thrust us back into the aboriginal wastes of the warring
heathen, have an overwhelming immediacy. An unerring tact
led Tennyson to separate these laureate verses from the
poem proper, and they now stand on either side of the
Idylls like incongruous fragments from a lesser world.[16]

II · Evolving the Form

"Perfection in art," Tennyson remarked, "is perhaps more sudden sometimes than we think; but then the long preparation for it, that unseen germination, *that* is what we ignore and forget."[1] The unseen germination of the *Idylls of the King* goes back at least to that moment in Tennyson's early youth when he first read Malory and "the vision of Arthur as I have drawn him . . . had come upon me."[2] The vision remained with him until his death, within a few months of which he made the last of the innumerable revisions of the *Idylls*. As Kathleen Tillotson observes, the poem, which is so richly concerned with time and change, was itself subject in the long course of its composition to the pressures of time and change.[3]

Yet despite its tortuous evolution, the *Idylls* displays a remarkable unity. The germ of the whole, the fragmentary "Morte d'Arthur," drafted in 1833, revised in 1835, and published in 1842, was so instinctually right in tone and design that over a quarter of a century after its first publication Tennyson could incorporate it without change into the still-unfinished *Idylls* of 1869. During the next two decades he continually altered and expanded the design of the larger poem without violating the verbatim integrity of this first-composed but last-in-sequence of the idylls. With the hindsight the completed poem grants us, we can see that this

last of the idylls had to come first, or at least that no other
segment of the Arthurian cycle could have fit with fewer
complications into Tennyson's ultimate design. At this stage
in the decline of the Round Table, the cast of characters has
dwindled to Arthur and the sole surviving knight who
witnesses his passing, and the overriding theme of the
poem—the wasting away of human aspiration in the face
of time—is felt at its keenest. Drawn to that part of the
Arthurian myth which most compelled his imagination,
Tennyson begins abruptly upon a conjunction—"So all day
long the noise of battle rolled"—which implies everything
that comes before it yet leaves him the maximum freedom in
later developing the full story.[4]

In 1833 the coincidence of a personal catastrophe with
what can only be described as a lifelong obsession led
Tennyson to begin his two "Arthur" poems, the "Morte
d'Arthur" and *In Memoriam*. The obsession concerned some
apocalyptic upheaval—of a city, a civilization, of the earth
itself—and is present in Tennyson's earliest writing. The
catastrophe was the sudden death of Arthur Hallam, the
news of which reached Tennyson on October 1, 1833, and his
response to which he made public seventeen years later in
In Memoriam. The "Morte d'Arthur" was as much a reaction
to the actual Arthur's death as was *In Memoriam*. The
earliest manuscript fragments of the two poems appear in
the same notebook, and Tennyson himself strongly hints at
their common origin in the autobiographical "Merlin and
the Gleam" (1889):

> Clouds and darkness
> Closed upon Camelot;
> Arthur had vanished
> I knew not whither,
> The king who loved me,
> And cannot die . . .

(st. VII)

The king who "loved *me*" and cannot die is clearly Arthur Hallam, yet he is also the Arthur of the *Idylls*.[5] The two are virtually indistinguishable: "Thou art the highest and most human too," Guinevere says of her king (G, 644); and Tennyson addresses the king of *In Memoriam* as "Known and unknown; human, divine" (sec. CXXIX). Given the internal and external evidence, Sir Charles Tennyson's comment on the connection between Hallam's death and the "Morte d'Arthur" strikes me as indisputable: Tennyson in part "sublimate[d] in *Morte d'Arthur* his own passionate grief at the death of Arthur Hallam."* Beneath the measured cadences of Bedivere's lament for Arthur's passing, one senses the urgency of personal statement, as if Tennyson himself were forced to "go forth companionless" into an alien world. His profoundly personal quest for reunion with Hallam in *In Memoriam*—"Descend, and touch, and enter" (sec. XCIII)—becomes in the *Idylls* a profoundly impersonal despair for the passing not only of a hero but of civilization.

Haunted all his life by the ghosts of such passings, Tennyson was understandably drawn to the story of the doomed king who falls with the death of his kingdom. In his boyhood, before he had read Malory, Tennyson had written a whole series of poems whose titles alone betray his preoccupation with the subject: "The Fall of Jerusalem," "The Vale of Bones," "Babylon," "Lamentation of the Peruvians."[6] The Library of Trinity College, Cambridge, contains the manuscript of a poem far more ambitious than these which is remarkably premonitory of the apocalyptic close of the *Idylls*. Written when Tennyson was probably

---

* "The Idylls of the King," *The Twentieth Century*, 161 (1957), 279. In this connection, Tennyson's comment on the date at which he resolved to write a long poem on King Arthur takes on a special significance: "When I was twenty-four I meant to write a whole great poem on it, and began it in the 'Morte d'Arthur.'" Tennyson turned twenty-four in the year of Hallam's death. (See W. J. Rolfe, ed., *The Poetic and Dramatic Works of Alfred, Lord Tennyson* [Boston and New York, Houghton Mifflin, 1898], p. 849.)

not more than fifteen, "Armageddon" draws in its climactic passage upon the chapter in Revelation (16) in which the angels of the Lord pour out His wrath upon mankind on the Day of Judgment. The confused shoutings and "dark terrific pall" that obscure the battle of the Last Day in "Armageddon" also mark Arthur's last dim battle in the West. And the "dim cries / . . . As of some lonely city sacked by night" that accompany Arthur's passing echo the passage in "Armageddon" in which is heard

> the long low moaning
> Of inarticulate thunder like the wail
> Of some lost City in it's [sic] evil day.[7]

The pervasiveness of the apocalytic mode of vision throughout Tennyson's works has never been sufficiently appreciated. Previsions of some fiery fall—of Troy in "Oenone," of Camelot throughout the *Idylls*, of the earth itself in the early and astonishing "Kraken"[8]—are among the most striking motifs in his verse. The "annihilating anarchy" of "Armageddon" reappears near the end of *In Memoriam*, where the ice-capped mountains topple,

> And molten up, and roar in flood;
>   The fortress crashes from on high,
>   The brute earth lightens to the sky,
> And the great Aeon sinks in blood.[9]
>
> (sec. CXXVII)

This same apocalyptic landscape reappears in the great close of the *Idylls*, where Arthur moves his host by night

> Back to the sunset bound of Lyonnesse—
> A land of old upheaven from the abyss
> By fire, to sink into the abyss again;
> Where fragments of forgotten peoples dwelt,
> And the long mountains ended in a coast

Of ever-shifting sand, and far away
The phantom circle of a moaning sea.*

(PA, 81–87)

The image of some catastrophic upheaval figures crucially in Tennyson's earliest outline of an Arthurian poem. The sketch is remarkable in that it contains no narrative action whatsoever, yet its very stasis foreshadows one of the central symbols of the *Idylls*, the towering, illusory city poised on the brink of the abyss:

On the latest limit of the West in the land of Lyonnesse, where . . . all is now wild sea, rose the sacred Mount of Camelot. It rose from the deeps with gardens and bowers and palaces, and at the top of the Mount was King Arthur's hall, and the holy Minster with the Cross of gold. Here dwelt the King in glory apart, while the Saxons whom he had overthrown in twelve battles ravaged the land, and ever came nearer and nearer.
The Mount was the most beautiful in the world, sometimes green and fresh in the beam of morning, sometimes all one splendour, folded in the golden mists of the West. But all underneath it was hollow, and the mountain trembled, when the seas rushed bellowing through the porphyry caves; and there ran a prophecy that the mountain and the city on some wild morning would topple into the abyss and be no more . . .[10]

The hollowness of the mountain figures in the finished *Idylls* as the mists which enshroud the sacred Mount and

* Christopher Ricks points out that this line, so apt in its context of moaning warriors and ghostly king, was in fact composed some thirty-five years before its first publication in "The Passing of Arthur." The line was originally part of a canceled stanza of "How often, when a child, I lay reclined" (1833), was then printed in a trial edition of *The Lover's Tale*, suppressed a second time, and finally published in the 1869 edition of the *Idylls*. Again one is struck by the consistency of Tennyson's preoccupations, which impelled him to brood for half a lifetime until he had created a fitting context for an image that haunted him. See Christopher Ricks, "Tennyson's Methods of Composition," *Proceedings of the British Academy*, 52 (1966), 218–219.

symbolizes the whole series of interlocking illusions and betrayals that finally bring Camelot down in flames. Tennyson remains true to this earliest image of a fair appearance succumbing to a fatal reality, but his conception of Arthur "dwelling in glory apart" undergoes a significant change. The isolated Arthur of the prose sketch recalls one aspect of Tennyson himself in the 1830's, torn between his attraction to the "golden mists" of the imagination and the claims of social responsibility (the ever-encroaching Saxons). The Arthur of the *Idylls*, however, must abandon the "Palace of Art" in order to do the work of this world. Yet the "many-corridored complexities" of Camelot (MV, 730) also enshrine the aesthetic imagination, which Tennyson felt was threatened by the rationalist-materialist bias of his age. In reanimating the myth of Arthur he was deliberately trying to conserve ancient modes of thought and feeling that he knew to be vital not only to his private activity as a poet but to the continuity of our culture. This conviction informs the close of the very early "Timbuctoo,"[11] in which the Spirit of Fable praises

> The permeating life which courseth through
> All the intricate and labyrinthine veins
> Of the great vine of *Fable*, which, outspread
> With growth of shadowing leaf and clusters rare,
> Reacheth to every corner under Heaven,
> Deep-rooted in the living soil of truth.
>
> (216–221)

The Spirit surveys the splendid domes and gardens of a city that symbolizes the poetic imagination, and laments that they must all soon fall victim

> To keen *Discovery:* soon yon brilliant towers
> Shall darken with the waving of her wand;
> Darken, and shrink and shiver into huts,
> Black specks amid a waste of dreary sand,

Low-built, mud-walled, Barbarian settlements.
How changed from this fair City!

(240–245)

The fall of this fair city of the imagination is one of the
most striking anticipations in Tennyson's early verse of the
fall of Camelot; in both "Timbuctoo" and the *Idylls* the
"brilliant towers" of the mind's own building give way to a
desolate, post-civilized landscape of forgotten peoples and
waste sands.

I have tried to suggest why Tennyson's imagination was so
strongly predisposed to the story of Arthur, and why in
the year of Hallam's death he was moved to begin his first
major poem on what he called "the greatest of all poetical
subjects."[12] It remains for us to see how, having found his
subject, he reshaped it in the light of his own genius.

A clue to Tennyson's earliest intentions appears in the
introductory verses to the "Morte d'Arthur," where we learn
that the poet has burnt his epic on "King Arthur, some
twelve books," for they were mere "faint Homeric echoes,
nothing-worth." Only the "Morte" was plucked from the
flames in the conviction that "its use will come." The
imaginary burning of the books is more than a device for
introducing, in medias res, the isolated fragment on Arthur's
passing.[13] It symbolizes Tennyson's rejection, sometime
between the drafting of the "Morte" in 1833 and its
publication nine years later, of an epic model for the *Idylls*.
"At twenty-four I meant to write an epic or drama of King
Arthur," he remarked after the *Idylls* was nearly completed:
"I said I should do it in twenty years; but the Reviews
stopped me." Hypersensitive to criticism, Tennyson was
doubtless distressed by the mixed reviews of the "Morte";[14]
if they in fact stopped him, one can only be grateful. Eleven
more books in the ostensibly epic form of the "Morte" might
indeed have produced "Homeric echoes, nothing-worth."*

* That Tennyson describes the "Morte" as the *eleventh* book of the

As is, he began with that part of the Arthurian cycle which, together with "The Coming of Arthur," most lends itself to epic treatment: the national hero who creates a kingdom and dies in single combat in its defense. Tennyson himself pointed out that the form and style of these two frame poems are "purposely more archaic" than the ten Round Table idylls which they enclose.[15] Once the final design completed itself in his mind, he turned the initial disparity to aesthetic advantage. He added to the original epic fragment the great opening lines of "The Passing" (1–169) that draw together all the dominant symbols of the *Idylls*, thereby binding the "Morte" to all that precedes it. And by setting off from the Round Table idylls the paired poems which mark Arthur's coming into the mutable world and passing into another, Tennyson incorporates into the very structure of the *Idylls* its cyclic themes of change and permanence, of time and eternity.

Despite its evident excellence, one detects a certain unevenness in the "Morte." Its most moving moments are elegiac rather than epic, pictorial rather than narrative, such as Arthur's eulogy to his fallen knights or Bedivere's lament as he watches the barge vanish, knowing that he must

<blockquote>
. . . go forth companionless,
And the days darken round me, and the years,
Among new men, strange faces, other minds.
(PA, 404–406)
</blockquote>

One suspects that Tennyson's abandoned prose sketch, in which absolutely nothing happens but everything is seen with fixed intensity, was in fact closer to his essential genius

---

burned epic suggests that he may have originally intended to follow it, as Malory does, with Lancelot and Guinevere's renunciation of earthly love, their final interview at Almesbury, and their deaths. In the *Idylls*, Tennyson merely alludes earlier in the poem to these events, thus reserving "The Passing of Arthur" for the climactic position and closing the circle begun with "The Coming of Arthur."

than the more conventionally epic portions of the "Morte."
Yet the Arthurian story to which he had committed himself
was crowded with actions of all kinds, some suited to epic
treatment, such as Arthur's last battle, some to the highly
mannered conventions of romance, such as the tale of
Lancelot and Elaine, some to a more allegorical handling, such
as the story of Merlin and Vivien, which Tennyson recast
as a medieval debate of body and soul. The reviewers
doubtless slowed his progress, but the seventeen-year hiatus
between the publication of the "Morte" and that of the first
four idylls of 1859 was due far more to Tennyson's uncertain
quest for a form that would encompass the inherent diversity
of his subject.[16]

In addition to the prose sketch for an Arthurian work,
Tennyson considered two other schemes, both fortunately
abandoned. One was for a drama or masque in five acts; the
scenario, with its projected "Chorus of Ladies of the Lake,"
disastrously suggests a sort of Christmas pantomime set
to music. The second, more fragmentary outline calls for an
allegorical rendering in which Arthur is to stand for
"Religious Faith," Merlin for "Science," and the Round Table
for "liberal institutions."[17]

Although Tennyson very soon gave up the idea of
structuring the *Idylls* as a strict allegory, his commentators
persisted in interpreting the poem as such, provoking him to
remark: "They have taken my hobby, and ridden it too
hard, and have explained some things too allegorically,
although there is an allegorical or perhaps rather a parabolic
drift in the poem."[18] Tennyson appears to have been both
flattered by the finding of allegorical significances in the
Idylls and deeply apprehensive that such readings were
reductive of his whole intention. Hence his revealingly
ambiguous reply to those who asked whether or not the Three
Queens who appear at Arthur's coronation stand for Faith,
Hope, and Charity: "They are right, and they are not right.
They mean that and they do not. They are three of the

noblest of women. They are also those three Graces, but
they are much more. I hate to be tied down to say, 'This
means *that*,' because the thought within the image is much
more than any one interpretation."[19] By "parabolic drift"
and "thought within the image," Tennyson means precisely
what we mean by *symbol*, the antithesis of the reductive,
this-for-that equivalence which his commentators have found
in the *Idylls*. The point is not that allegory is simplistic—
a patent absurdity—but that the *Idylls* is not an allegory
and that those who so read it are forced into simplistic
conclusions.

Yet in a curiously conspiratorial way Tennyson encouraged
such misreadings: "By King Arthur I always meant the soul,
and by the Round Table the passions and capacities of
a man."[20] But if, as Tennyson writes in the Epilogue, the
Idylls is about "Sense at war with Soul," why is the "sinful"
Lancelot, usurper of the Soul's bed, the secular hero of the
poem? The answer lies in a confusion of intention in
Tennyson and of perception in his critics. An allegorical
residue remains embedded in the overall symbolic structure
of the poem, although only once—when Arthur ("Soul")
denounces Guinevere ("Sense")—does the mixture of modes
jar on the reader. Elsewhere, this residue results in a certain
deficiency of realization, as with the Lady of the Lake
or those

> three fair queens,
> Who stood in silence near his throne, the friends
> Of Arthur, gazing on him, tall, with bright
> Sweet faces, who will help him at his need.
> (CA, 275–278)

The difficulty with the trio is that they have no narrative
function and no real connection with the poem's central
characters or symbols, and so they stand in idle silence. They
are simply part of the magical donné of Arthurian legend,
to which Tennyson remains perhaps too diffidently faithful.

His awareness of this dilemma always shows itself in a failure in his craft as a poet: the verse either becomes portentous or,. as in the cited passage, lapses into the *contrivedly* prosaic (unlike Wordsworth, Tennyson is incapable of being unwittingly prosaic).

At the other extreme from an abstraction such as the Lady of the Lake ("The Church") are those characters who so richly embody the poem's moral and psychological complexities that any attempt to tag them with allegorical labels at once breaks down. Lancelot, for example, is larger than any didactic formula we might devise to contain him, and it is his greatness as a character that he compels us, in our attempts at explanation, to enlarge our terms of moral definition. His love for his king is as absolute as his love for his queen, and it is his tragedy that loyalty to one must be disloyalty to the other:

> The great and guilty love he bare the Queen,
> In battle with the love he bare his lord,
> Had marred his face, and marked it ere his time.
>
> (LE, 244–246)

The whole force of this passage lies in the juxtaposed "great *and* guilty": the guilt of the love is indisputable, but so too is its greatness, by which Tennyson means not only intensity but nobility. Indeed, the guilt is a function of the nobility; were it not for Lancelot's nobility, he would feel no guilt, and without the guilt, there would be less greatness. The paradox of the adultery of Lancelot and Guinevere is that it not only "mars" them (and the kingdom) but ultimately ennobles them (and the kingdom), as Tennyson emphasizes by contrast with another adulterous triangle— the guiltless, peculiarly modern and joyless affair of Tristram and Isolt.

Yet in a recent book on the *Idylls* we read that Lancelot's guilty love of Guinevere "has coarsened not only his moral sensibilities but also his appearance." [21] Nothing could more

starkly illustrate the pitfalls consequent upon reading the
Idylls as a war of Sense versus Soul, in which certain
characters represent the vices of the first and others the
virtues of the second. The warfare, as James D. Merriman
has brilliantly shown, "is not between individuals, but rather
within individuals, and the various characters in the *Idylls*
illustrate at any given time some stage of victory or defeat
in that inner struggle." [22] Gawain's losing inner battle
exactly parallels the outer struggle of the kingdom. His
progressive degeneration from idyll to idyll is so beautifully
integrated with that of the realm, from its founding in the
spring to its barren end in the winter, that we scarcely notice
him, for the changes in the character's moral foliation all but
merge with those of the kingdom. Lancelot's far more
tempestuous struggle moves in the opposite direction, toward
salvation, and even those characters at the moral extremes
of humanity—the harlot Vivien, for example—have an
energy and solidity that elude any reductive personification
such as "The Flesh." Only Galahad stands outside the arena
of moral combat, and his victory over the flesh, as Merriman
points out, "comes at the expense of simply abandoning the
world, the real battleground of the war between Sense
and Soul." [23]

The *Idylls* dramatizes on all levels the only conflict that
can engage the mature moral imagination—the clash not of
right versus wrong but of right versus right. Allegorical
interpretations of the *Idylls* obscure this distinction and
substitute didactic solutions for the moral dilemmas it poses.
Thus one critic assures us that the *Idylls* represents the
triumph of "the high soul of man" over the passions, while
another describes the poem as an allegory of the collapse
which "must follow the rejection of spiritual values." [24] Yet
the moral of the *Idylls* is not that men must abide by spiritual
values, any more than the moral of *Othello* is that wives
should look to their linen. In this sense, the poem is totally
without a moral but explores instead the ambiguous results

of man's quest for such values, and the disastrous effects of abandoning them. In "Lancelot and Elaine" *denial* of the flesh proves fatal, and as "The Holy Grail" makes clear, spiritual values can drive men as mad as sexual obsession. Tennyson suggests a possible connection between the two: the color red, which throughout the *Idylls* symbolizes sexuality, is also associated with the Grail itself, first seen as "rose-red" by a nun in a condition of erotic ecstasy, then as "blood-red" by Galahad—as is fitting for the vessel that bore Christ's blood.

Even of this simplest of the poem's thematic antitheses— white as purity, red as passion—we cannot say "*this* means *that*." The lily maid of Astolat, white in purity, is at first glance a personification of Virgin Innocence; but her dreams are insistently sexual and the sleeve she gives Lancelot is scarlet, for her purity, like the nun's, is profoundly passionate. Because the lily maid is not a conventional figure in an allegory, our impulse is to distort her into a modern simplism of our own: seeming purity masking a libidinous reality. Yet like the symbols associated with her, she is neither this nor that, but both pure *and* passionate, sexual *and* innocent, embodying the same intense conjunction of contrary elements that draws her instantly—and fatally— to Lancelot.

In 1859, when "Lancelot and Elaine" was published, Tennyson for the first time grouped his new series of Arthurian poems under the general title *Idylls of the King*.[25] An idyll is a "little picture" of a character or mood colored by a single, dominant emotion. Tennyson's choice of the plural *idylls* stresses his intention, as Jerome Buckley points out, to portray "not a single unified narrative but a group of chivalric tableaux selected from a great mass of available legend . . . Each of the Idylls moves through a series of sharply visualized vignettes toward its pictured climax, its moment of revelation."[26] Yet true as this is, one's experience of the *Idylls* is less static than it suggests. The sharply

visualized vignettes which characterize so much of the poem
—Lancelot kneeling before Guinevere in the vine-clad oriel
window, Balin and Balan "sitting statue-like" by the
fountain—are not simply pictures but *actions*, or rather their
pictorial intensity is so great that we experience them as
actions. The very early "Mariana" consists entirely of this
hypercharged description. Imprisoned in her moated grange,
Mariana is an animate extension of the setting, the setting
a symbolic embodiment of her mental entrapment. The
Idylls is filled with such moments of fixed intensity in which
the energy of outward action turns in upon itself and
narration becomes a kind of dramatized vision. The first
critic to perceive this quality in Tennyson's verse was Arthur
Hallam, and there is a certain ghostly aptness in summoning
Hallam to illuminate the poetry in which he later figures so
largely. Reviewing the volume in which "Mariana" first
appeared, Hallam remarks on Tennyson's

power of embodying himself in . . . moods of character,
with such extreme accuracy of adjustment, that the
circumstances of the narration seem to have a natural
correspondence with the predominant feeling, and, as it were,
to be evolved from it by assimilative force . . . These
expressions of character are brief and coherent: nothing
extraneous to the dominant fact is admitted, nothing
illustrative of it, and, as it were, growing out of it, is rejected.
They are like summaries of mighty dramas . . . We contend
that it is a new species of poetry, a graft of the lyric on the
dramatic.[27]

Although the phrase was not in Hallam's vocabulary, he
comes astonishingly close to saying in 1831 what we are only
now recognizing in the 1970's: Tennyson is essentially a
symbolist poet. Donald Smalley has noted the anomalous
fact that while on one side of the Channel middle-class
Victorians were finding the *Idylls* congenial to their taste, on
the opposite shore the poem was being appreciated by an
audience that "the Laureate would scarcely have anticipated

or been likely to welcome—the French Symbolists." The
influence of Tennyson on Poe ("I regard him as the noblest
poet who ever lived") and, through Poe, on Baudelaire and
Mallarmé constitutes one of the vital currents flowing into the
poetry of our century. Mallarmé translated "Mariana,"
Baudelaire borrowed from Tennyson, and Yeats, who read
Hallam's essay in the 1890's, found it indispensable to an
understanding of the French Symbolists.[28]

The symbolist technique that Hallam recognized in
"Mariana" reaches its furthest development in the *Idylls*.
The solitary Elaine in her tower, dreaming of Lancelot and
stripping the silken case from his naked shield, is a more
complex version of Mariana in her moated grange.
Tennyson's whole problem in structuring the *Idylls* consisted
in getting Elaine, as it were, down from her tower and onto
the poem's field of action. A long narrative poem made up
of separate vignettes, however sharply visualized, would
collapse of its own static weight. Tennyson solved the
problem by incorporating individual characters into the larger
landscape of the *Idylls*; as in "Mariana," he obliterates the
gap between self and scene and frees himself from bondage
to conventional narrative. Building on the techniques of the
classical idyll, with its intensification of mood, its highly
allusive texture, its startling juxtapositions, flashbacks, and
deliberate discontinuities, Tennyson creates an inclusive
psychological landscape in which all the separate
consciousnesses in the poem participate and in which each
action is bound to all others through symbol, prophecy, or
retrospect.[29]

Seen from this perspective, the first lines Tennyson
composed for the *Idylls* take on a singular significance. The
"Morte" begins with the simplest and apparently slightest
of alterations from Malory:

So all day long the noise of battle rolled
Among the mountains by the *winter* sea . . .

Tennyson's shift in the setting of Arthur's death from
summer to winter suggests that from the start he had in
mind the symbolic season in whose cycle of florescence and
decline every scene and character in the *Idylls* is enmeshed.
It is impossible to exaggerate the fullness of consequence this
single alteration bears. Throughout Malory, with the
exception of the closing chapters, one feels the suspension of
time characteristic of romance. In such a world everything
is possible, coincidence abounds, and spring is eternal. Only
in "Gareth and Lynette," the first of the Round Table
idylls, does Tennyson allow his reader this primal fantasy
of romance. By linking the separate idylls to the cycle of
seasons, Tennyson transposes the dominant mode
of Arthurian myth from romance to tragedy, in which
the only release from time is death.

The symbolic season, then, enabled Tennyson to control
the random, timeless sequence of events in Malory.* In the

* In comparing Tennyson and Malory I am aware of the difficulty of
avoiding invidiousness. Perhaps the most nearly neutral formulation
would be that Malory is a great story-teller and Tennyson a great poet,
and that Tennyson's departures from the *Morte d'Arthur* are largely
a consequence of this difference. Tennyson selects and compresses
where Malory can afford to be diffuse; Malory is rapid and encyclopedic
where Tennyson is elaborate, yet intense. Malory's characters are in
constant motion, camping and decamping, love-making, marching
and jousting. Tennyson's characters do all of these things but also
reflect upon them. They seem less like anonymous figures rushing
headlong through a landscape than extensions of the landscape itself,
which they in turn animate with their own natures. Malory's characters
inhabit a simpler world of heroic action. Tennyson's characters
inhabit the more familiar world of divided wills and anguished
introspection; they are ourselves, veiled in mist.

Where Malory has most mastered his materials, Tennyson follows
him most closely, as in "The Passing of Arthur" and the finely-wrought
tale of Lancelot and Elaine. Where Malory appears lost in the
prolixity of his own sources, as in the wearisome account of Arthur's
Roman wars, Tennyson drastically compresses him. In certain idylls,
most notably "Guinevere," he freely invents, and for the two Geraint
idylls he uses Lady Charlotte Guest's translation of the *Mabinogion*,
his only major source other than Malory. Throughout the *Morte*

Morte d'Arthur, for example, the tragedy of Balin and Balan precedes the romance of Gareth and Lynette. Tennyson reverses the order of the two tales, as elsewhere he compresses the more diffuse episodes in Malory or cuts them altogether.[30] What remains of this distillation from the *Morte d'Arthur* Tennyson orders along a strict narrative sequence in which the clock of Arthur's fall ticks at a steadily accelerating rate. Yet this *linear* movement through time, while it lends a propulsive thrust to the narrative, tends to make of each idyll a separate episode spaced out along the temporal chain. And so Tennyson superimposes upon this strict chronological sequence a much more fluid temporal movement in which events that are narratively sequential appear to take place simultaneously in the reader's mind. Thus although "Balin and Balan" comes quite early in the chronological sequence and is set in the time of the lady-fern and the lily, we are made to feel a sudden acceleration of the symbolic season, in consonance with this first of the idylls that ends tragically. By implying early in "Balin and Balan" that Arthur's youth has passed, Tennyson ages his hero and the kingdom in a single line:

> Early, one fair dawn,
> The light-winged spirit of his youth *returned . . .*
>   (18–19, italics added)

---

d'Arthur one senses a certain unsureness of control, with the central story of King Arthur and his Round Table slipping in and out of focus. Too often the hundreds of encounters of knights in combat—first on horseback, then unhorsed, then hand to hand, each contest ever so slightly varied from the last—take on the peculiar unreality of multiple copulations in a modern best-seller, endless variations in erotic posture currently gratifying a taste akin to that for the never-ending joust in medieval romance. Tennyson's genius in giving coherence to the inherent diffuseness of Arthurian romance can only be appreciated by going back to his sources and seeing, retrospectively, how he has breathed life and depth into the mass of intransigent matter on which he drew. Guilty neither of slavish imitation nor of mindless license, he perceived the "fine things" in Malory but also saw that they were "loosely strung together without art." (Cited in Christopher Ricks, ed., *The Poems of Tennyson* [London, Longmans, 1969], p. 1460.)

The very brevity and symmetry of "Balin and Balan"—it is less than half as long as "Gareth and Lynette," one third as long as the Geraint idylls that precede it—reinforce this sense of propulsive doom.

Tennyson's manipulation of time in the *Idylls* produces an effect akin to that of syncopation in music or, closer to his medium, to departures from regular meter in a line of verse. When the stress falls unexpectedly, it falls with twice the weight. The annual Tournament of Diamonds, spaced over nine years, establishes the normal temporal rhythm of the poem. But in "The Holy Grail," when the knights seek violent escape from the diurnal world to the world of eternity, Tennyson causes time to run amok: the narrative is deliberately discontinuous and kaleidoscopic; lightning and darkness, droughts and floods, replace any recognizable moment of day or year; apocalyptic time—in which all times are simultaneously present—displaces chronological time.

Throughout the *Idylls* leitmotifs of all kinds cut across the linear narrative and connect past and future. "Merlin and Vivien" opens with an impending storm that finally bursts in the closing lines; recurrent images of tempests and waves gather to a climax the storm of warring passions internalized in Merlin and externalized in nature. Before Vivien seduces him, indeed before the "present" in which the idyll is narrated, Merlin has

> walked with dreams and darkness, and he found
> A doom that ever poised itself to fall,
> An ever-moaning battle in the mist,
> World-war of dying flesh against the life.
> (188–191)

The wave poised to break symbolizes the seer's prevision of his own doom, but his fall is both a cause and prophecy of the larger fall of the kingdom. And so the dreams and darkness through which he walked later become the clouds of self-doubt that enshroud Arthur at the end; the moaning struggle in the mist foreshadows the last dim battle in the West, when the "wave" of heathen at last engulfs the kingdom, and it reverberates back to the founding, when Arthur pushed back the heathen wave and "made a realm and reigned" (CA, 518).

Like each of the idylls, "Merlin and Vivien" tells a self-contained story that is also interwoven into the central story of Arthur's coming and passing. Through dreams, prophecy, and retrospect, through recurrent symbols, characters, settings, and verbal echoes, any part of the poem implies all other parts. Guinevere's marriage vow to Arthur, itself ironic—"King and my lord, I love thee to the death!" (CA, 469)—is ironically echoed much later by the vow of Tristram to Isolt:

> Come, I am hungered and half-angered—meat,
> Wine, wine—and I will love thee to the death—
> (LT, 713–714)

a lie made true by Tristram's murder the instant after it is sworn, as Guinevere's lie is finally proven true by her repentance in the convent of Almesbury.

The major characters reappear from idyll to idyll, forming a "human chain of kinship"[31] whose linkages serve the same unifying function as the poem's clusters of symbols. Minor characters who appear only once, or rarely, are in turn incorporated into the larger story by a kind of analogical patterning through which one character reenacts the role previously played by another. The early idylls present special problems of narrative continuity, for happy endings are by definition self-contained, as the tag-phrase "they lived happily ever after" makes clear.[32] "Gareth and Lynette" has just such an ending: Gareth's fearsome adversaries prove to be mock-monsters in disguise, and the novice knight wins the scornful lady. "Pelleas and Ettarre" tells the same story in reverse,[33] the later idyll retrospectively enriching the earlier. Fair appearance conceals a hideous reality, and the sadistic Ettarre drives the young Pelleas impotent and mad. Gareth tests and finds himself at a time when the integrity of the kingdom and his own naive idealism are in perfect accord. Pelleas is Gareth reborn in decadent times; the clash between his idealism and the corruption of the kingdom destroys him, for he can find no supporting matrix for his fledgling identity. "What name hast thou?" Lancelot asks as Pelleas bears down upon him in blind rage. "No name, no name," he shouts, "I am wrath and shame and hate and evil fame" (551–556).

As certain characters seem to exchange identities, so certain settings recur throughout the *Idylls.* Early in "Balin and Balan," for example, Balin observes a meeting between Lancelot and Guinevere in a garden of roses and lilies. The queen walks down the path of roses toward Lancelot but he pauses in his greeting, for he has dreamed the previous night of "That maiden Saint who stands with lily in hand / In yonder shrine" (256–257), and the dream restrains him, just as his praise of the perfect purity of the lilies chills Guinevere:

> "Sweeter to me," she said, "this garden rose
> Deep-hued and many-folded! sweeter still
> The wild-wood hyacinth and the bloom of May.
> Prince, we have ridden before among the flowers
> In those fair days—not as cool as these,
> Though season-earlier."
>
> (264–268)

Guinevere nowhere more richly expresses the sensuousness which first drew Lancelot to her than in these lines, "deep-hued and many-folded." The consequences of that first, fatally joyous meeting reverberate throughout the poem, as here, when the sight of the lovers shocks Balin into his former "violences," and he rides off from the orderly garden into the wilderness where he meets his death. The garden scene works perfectly within the narrative of "Balin and Balan" at the same time that it takes us back, through Guinevere's reminiscence, to the time before the founding of the Round Table and forward to "Lancelot and Elaine." The scene opens out to become the entire settling of the later idyll, in which Lancelot again must walk the same divided path and choose between the rose of Guinevere and the lily-maid of Astolat.

In the light of such subtle architectonics one is at a loss to understand much of the twentieth-century criticism of the *Idylls*: "Utterly wanting in unity and coherence of structure . . . strikingly uneven . . . a collection of episodes . . . Tennyson could not tell a story at all . . . he failed signally to bring out the underlying, archetypical significance of the ancient mythological symbols he was employing."[34] Tennyson could of course tell a story perfectly well. He handles the conventional narrative devices with virtuousity, ranging from the first-person monologue of Percivale in "The Holy Grail" to the omniscient narrator in "Lancelot and Elaine," from the simple plot of "Merlin and Vivien" to the complex interweavings of the two adulterous triangles in "The Last Tournament." Yet however skillfully he might retell the tales in Malory or the *Mabinogion*, he would end where he began, with "a collection of episodes." And so he developed, in Hallam's phrase, "a new species of poetry" in order to convey his vision of Arthurian myth to the contemporary world. Like every great long poem, the *Idylls* draws on traditional forms and is itself a new genre. Shakespeare had Seneca and Marlowe; Milton had Homer; but tragedy and epic radically redefine themselves in their works. Tennyson bears this same innovative relation to tradition, but we have yet to assimilate into our literature this poem which is at once epic and lyric, narrative and drama, tragedy and romance. Our difficulty with Tennyson's "medieval charade" is not its derivativeness but its novelty.

III · Timescape

The *Idylls of the King* was written during a period when man's sense of time was undergoing a change as radical as that effected in his sense of space by Copernicus three centuries earlier. First geology and then evolution pushed back the origins of things from the imagined instant of Creation to unimaginably remote beginnings; and the imminent Last Day opened out upon eonian cycles of days without end. Had it not been for Lyell and Darwin, the *Idylls* would have had shorter temporal vistas, and Tennyson could neither have written nor described it as the history not of a single man or generation "but of a whole cycle of generations."[1] Tennyson, like Donne before him, made poetry out of the "new science."

Frank Kermode speculates that this enlarged sense of time is causally linked to the development of the novel. One regrets that in his gnomically brilliant *Sense of an Ending* he does not glance at the *Idylls,* which makes a highly novelistic use of time. If, in Rossetti's phrase, the sonnet is a "moment's monument," then the traditional novel is the chronicle of a generation, and the *Idylls* of a whole civilization. Unlike the sonnet, the novel and the long narrative poem have a felt duration in time; we take so many hours to get through them, and the realism we sense in the novel stems in part from the felt consonance between the real time we invest in the reading and the fictional time vicariously experienced in the aging of the characters. Tennyson grafted onto the long poem the temporal richness characteristic of the novel, borrowing his time-scale from Darwin and his cast from Arthurian romance.

The blurring of the comfortingly finite limits of biblical time accounts for much of the anxiety reflected in Victorian literature, from Dickens' lost orphans to the terror-ridden narrator in James Thomson's "City of Dreadful Night." Tennyson's prayer in *In Memoriam*—"Be near me when my light is low"—is a classic expression of the anxiety associated not merely with the withdrawal of God but with the secularizing and dehumanizing of time, which he characterizes as "a maniac scattering dust" (sec. L). The medieval revival attempted to rediscover—or invent—a world outside the unending flux and reflux of the new time. It is one of the ironies of the *Idylls*, itself a product of the medieval revival, that it invests Arthurian legend with all the bad tidings of the new sciences.

In *In Memoriam* Hallam is the "herald of a higher race," a "noble type" of perfected man (sec. CXVIII; Epilogue); in the *Idylls*, through a cataclysmic reversal of evolution, men "reel back into the beast." Evolution has been tinged with Apocalypse. A couplet from "Locksley Hall Sixty Years After" epitomizes the antiphonal connection between the two poems:

Evolution ever climbing after some ideal good,
And Reversion ever dragging Evolution in the mud.
                                                    (199–200)

In mid-Victorian England, despite nature red in tooth and claw, Tennyson could still link the myth of progress to evolutionary theory and see in both the fulfillment of that "one far-off divine event" when men, having evolved into gods, will "live in God" (*In Memoriam*, Epilogue). As the century approached its end, the temporal vistas took on a progressively more frightening aspect, and ancient modes of apprehending time resurfaced. The malaise associated with the *fin de siècle* is only the most recent of successive periods of terror projected upon the ends of centuries and felt with particular force on the eve of the millennial year 1000. This anxiety was clearly resurgent at the end of the nineteenth century; the *fin de siècle* served as a type of the *fin du monde*.[2] That three of the most notable long poems in the latter part of the nineteenth century—"The Wreck of the Deutschland," "The City of Dreadful Night," and the *Idylls of the King*—are apocalyptic in design and imagery is no more coincidental than that Yeats, who came to maturity at this time, should be the great modern poet of Apocalypse. "The blood-dimmed tide is loosed" might serve as an epigraph for the *Idylls*, and Christ the Rough Beast slouching toward Bethlehem is the perfect heraldic emblem for Arthur's last battle, itself an image of the end of the world.

Of course Tennyson's darker visions did not require a *fin de siècle* stimulus; they were there from the beginning, as "Armageddon" makes clear. But I think it beyond dispute that the *Idylls* takes on the somber coloring of the century's close, exactly as the clear skies of Ruskin's *Modern Painters* (written, like *In Memoriam*, in mid-century) darken in his late, apocalyptic *Storm Cloud of the Nineteenth Century* (1884). Sir Charles Tennyson describes his grandfather's temper of mind in 1886, just after he had published the last of the idylls:

His natural tendency to gloom and despondency reasserted itself and he became more and more oppressed with doubts about the usefulness of his own work and the future of humanity. He was more than ever obsessed by the thought that the world was standing on the brink of a revolution such as had never been seen before—"a last dim battle in the West" which, if it came, would be world wide.

"When I see society vicious and the poor starving in great cities," he said, "I feel that it is a mighty wave of evil passing over the world, but that there will be yet some new and strange development which I shall not live to see . . . You must not be surprised at anything that comes to pass in the next fifty years. All ages are ages of transition, but this is an awful moment of transition . . . The truth is that the wave advances and recedes . . . I tried in my 'Idylls' to teach men the need of the ideal, but I feel sometimes as if my life had been a very useless life."[3]

The two kinds of time that I have been discussing—cyclic and apocalyptic—are built into the structure of the *Idylls*. The first is epitomized in the best-known and least understood line of the poem, stated at its opening and repeated like a closing chord at the end: "The old order changeth, yielding place to new" (CA, 508; PA, 408). The line itself constitutes a profoundly ambiguous cycle recapitulating the larger, dynastic cycles of the poem: first Rome, "the slowly-fading mistress of the world" (CA, 504), yields to the barbarians, who are then subdued by Arthur, who in turn yields to the chaos that succeeds him. If the first use of the line seems to promise perpetual renewal, its repetition implies the reverse. For Arthur's "new order" at the opening has become the "old order" at the end, and the order that replaces Arthur is even more barbarous than the one he displaced.

From this cyclic perspective, man's reeling back into the beast is both monstrous and *natural*. The Round Table is founded to arrest this process, and it succeeds only "for a space." The time before and after Arthur, and of all the later idylls except "The Holy Grail," is cyclic time, or time in nature, as opposed to Arthur's time, which is eternity and is always rendered apocalyptically. Of the several intentionally conflicting accounts of Arthur's birth and parentage in "The Coming of Arthur," one is especially relevant here. We learn from Bellicent, who long ago heard from Bleys, the master of Merlin, that Arthur was born on a dismal, storm-tossed night "in which the bounds of heaven and earth were lost" (371). The narrative is deliberately couched in indirection, for Tennyson is handling with great tact the central mystery of the *Idylls*, the dual nature of Arthur, who exists in time and transcends time. This is the moment of his "incarnation," and the storm over Tintagil which obscures the horizon symbolizes the instant when the temporal and the eternal transect.

The topography of Tintagil is itself emblematic of the rift in time associated with Arthur's birth. Bleys and Merlin pass through the castle gate and traverse a *chasm* dividing the land from the sea, where on the crest of a flaming wave they find the infant Arthur (369–383). Just as the margin separating heaven and earth is obscured, so fire and water are intermixed, the four elements mirroring in their confusion the breach in the normal temporal order. Bedivere, in keeping with his blunt simplicity, tells a less magical tale but it enforces the same point: on the night of the new year "*all before his time* / Was Arthur born" (210–211, italics added). Tennyson's intention here is underscored by his departure from the *Morte d'Arthur*, in which Arthur's birth occurs after the normal term and at an unspecified season. Tennyson breaks the biological cycle; he links both Arthur's birth and his death to the symbolic season, shifting Arthur's passing from summer to

> that day when the great light of heaven
> Burned at his lowest in the rolling year.
>
> (PA, 90–91)

Further, as J. M. Gray observes, Arthur's birth now accords with the season of the Epiphany;[4] the analogy with Christ's birth is subtle but unmistakable.

The same transection recurs in "The Coming of Arthur" as Bellicent describes the founding of the Round Table:

> Then the King in low deep tones,
> And simple words of great authority,

Bound them by so strait vows to his own self,
That when they rose, knighted from kneeling, some
Were pale as at the passing of a ghost,
Some flushed, and others dazed, as one who wakes
Half-blinded at the coming of a light.

(259–265)

The knights are in a state of shock, for the "so strait vows"
momentarily wrench them out of nature, and a "likeness of
the King" flashes "from eye to eye through all their Order"
(269–270). As God created man in His own image, so the
King, always associated with light, re-creates the knights in
his image. Although Tennyson never forces the analogy
between Christ and Arthur, it is ever present just below the
surface: "The King will follow Christ, and we the King,"
the knights sing at the close of "The Coming of Arthur,"
and at the start of the next idyll Gareth praises the King as
"the great Sun of Glory" (GL, 22). When Lancelot,
disclaiming that he is worthy of the young Lavaine's praise,
points to Arthur and says, "There is the man" (LE, 450),
Pilate's "Behold the man!" echoes with all its overtones of
betrayal in the reader's mind.[5] Arthur's coming is patterned
on the Incarnation; his passing, on the Passion. Between
the two, he founds a kind of secular church, the Round
Table, of which the knights are the communicants and the
vows the sacraments. "Man's word is God in man," Arthur
twice says, and the King is keeper of the Word (CA, 132;
BB, 8).

Arthur's time figures centrally in the two idylls which bear
his name and in which he is the chief actor. Cyclic time
figures centrally in the Round Table idylls, in which Arthur
is properly peripheral, a hovering presence rather than the
protagonist. Tennyson implies the distinction in his comment
on the "general drift" of the *Idylls:* "The whole is the
dream of man coming into practical life and ruined by one
sin. Birth is a mystery and death is a mystery, and in the
midst lies the tableland of life, and its struggles and

performances. It is not the history of one man or of one
generation but of a whole cycle of generations."[6] Within
this tableland one cycle is marked with especial clarity, the
period of Arthur's rule, which lasts for about twelve years.[7]
There are lesser cycles within this calendar of the reign,
such as the "twelvemonth and a day" of the Grail quest
(HG, 197). Before the birth of Arthur and the building of
Camelot lie the aboriginal past and the cycle of pagan Rome,
as after Arthur's fall lies the darkly indeterminate future.
All of these cycles exist in time, and together they constitute
the larger eon of man in nature; overarching them all is
eternity. Like Arthur, the "sacred mount of Camelot"
(HG, 227) symbolizes the juncture of the two great temporal
orders. From the perspective of natural time it is an illusion
in the mist; from the perspective of Arthur's time, it is
"built for ever" (GL, 274), though only intermittently visible
from "the tableland of life."

That tableland is pushed back to its furthest bounds in
"The Coming of Arthur." In the opening lines Tennyson
describes not only the origins of Arthur but those of the
human race. The rolling waves of blank verse carry us back
to a primordial waste in which men are as yet scarcely
differentiated from beasts:

> For many a petty king ere Arthur came
> Ruled in this isle, and ever waging war
> Each upon other, wasted all the land;
> And still from time to time the heathen host
> Swarmed overseas, and harried what was left.
> And so there grew great tracts of wilderness,
> Wherein the beast was ever more and more,
> But man was less and less, till Arthur came.
> 　　　　· · ·
> And after these King Arthur for a space,
> And through the puissance of his Table Round,
> Drew all their petty princedoms under him,
> Their king and head, and made a realm, and reigned.
> 　　　　　　　　　　　　　　　　　　(5–19)

Within this pre-Arthurian wilderness wild dogs and boars
root and wallow in the fields, and wolves lend their fierce
teats "to human sucklings" (23–29). Arthur figures in these
lines not as a fifth- or sixth-century chieftain, still less as a
medieval king, but as the culture-hero of myth who cleansed
the "dark land" and "slew the beast, and felled / The
forest, letting in the sun" (59–60). He is the bringer of
light and his reign is a kind of second Creation.

But Arthur's fragile experiment in civilization can only
"for a space" hold back the resurgence of the beasts, and even
this bright time of the founding is pregnant with the fall.
As Arthur and Guinevere leave their wedding chapel, the
altar blossoming with flowers, we scarcely notice the "Great
Lords from Rome" (476) who impatiently pace the ramparts
of the "city all on fire / With sun and cloth of gold"
(478–479). Their presence reminds us that just as Rome
has grown feeble and Arthur can spurn her demand for
tribute, so too the new kingdom will pass, but whereas Rome
is a "slowly-fading mistress" (504), Camelot will burst into
sudden flames, as the city "all on fire" ominously forebodes.*
This ambiguous conjunction of founding and fall recurs in
the strident coronation anthem which immediately follows
the marriage:

> Blow trumpet, for the world is white with May;
> Blow trumpet, the long night hath rolled away!
> Blow through the living world—"Let the King reign!"
> (481–483)

> Blow, for our Sun is mighty in his May!
> Blow, for our Sun is mightier day by day!
> Clang battleaxe, and clash brand! Let the King reign.
> (496–498)

* The city of burning gold is also a figure of the Heavenly City of
Revelation: "the city was pure gold . . . the glory of God did lighten it"
(21:18, 23). Throughout the *Idylls* Camelot has the dual aspect of
the New Jerusalem that rises in light and the Great Babylon that sinks
in flames.

Yet it is the nature of night to return, and if "our Sun" grows daily mightier in May, it will be dim indeed in the winter of the Last Battle, when the knights die to ghastly echoes of the coronation hymn:

> . . . the clash of brands, the crash
> Of battleaxes on shattered helms, and shrieks
> After the Christ.
>
> (PA, 109–111) [8]

Although the King is a Christ figure in origins, mission, and promise of his return, he is also a solar deity. Guinevere refers to him as "the Sun in heaven" (LE, 123), an apparent tautology that nicely capitalizes on the homonymic *Son* and *sun*. Arthur is so closely linked to the sun throughout the *Idylls* that his character never wholly detaches itself from the symbol, or the symbol from that ancient body of belief in which the gods, once housed in the heavens, descend to earth, are worshipped as heroes, and fructify the land. Underlying the medieval rites of the wedding of Arthur and Guinevere is the more primitive union of Sun and Earth.*

---

* Physical descriptions of Arthur stress his identification with light, gold, fire, and sun. In recounting the mystery of his origins to Leodogran, Bellicent observes "this king is fair / Beyond the race of Britons and of men" (CA, 329–330). Vivien speaks of his golden head and beard (BB, 505; MV, 58), one of the Three Queens describes the lustrous hair "that made his forehead like a rising sun" (PA, 385), and Tristram recalls the young king enthroned in splendor, "His hair, a sun that rayed from off a brow / Like hillsnow high in heaven" (LT, 661–662). Arthur lets in the sun, lightens the world, and at the taking of the vows his knights are "Half-blinded at the coming of a light" (CA, 60, 91–92, 265). He is born "clothed in fire" (CA, 389) and wields a sword "so bright / That men are blinded by it" (CA 299–300). He wears on his cuirass an emerald set in a radiant sun (LE, 293–295); on the field of the first battle "the fire of God" descends upon him, and "the Powers who walk the world / Made lightnings and great thunders over him / And dazed all eyes" (CA, 106–108).

The association of Guinevere with the earth is given prominence in the first lines of the *Idylls*, which begin, surprisingly, not with Arthur but with Leodogran's daughter, "fairest of all flesh on earth."

The marriage of the "great Sun of Glory" to the "fairest of all flesh on earth" (CA, 3) has a mythic residue reminiscent of that strange passage in Genesis in which the sons of God come in unto the daughters of men (6:4).

Prior to his marriage Arthur feels himself to be impotent and all but disembodied:

> . . . saving I be joined
> To her that is the fairest under heaven,
> I seem as nothing in the mighty world,
> And cannot work my will, nor work my work
> Wholly, nor make myself in mine own realm
> Victor and lord. But were I joined with her
> Then might we live together as one life,
> And reigning with one will in everything
> Have power on this dark land to lighten it,
> And power on this dead world to make it live.
>
> (CA, 84–93)

After the wedding Arthur's reign (unlike his sterile marriage) becomes fruitful and his power grows with the lengthening days. His career and that of the kingdom parallel not only the sun's annual cycle but the diurnal cycle from dawn to night. The briefer cycle is most clearly marked by Gareth's successive encounters with the four knights of the Morning

---

In Guinevere's phrase Arthur is "that pure severity of perfect light" (G, 641), whereas she yearns for the warmer tones of Lancelot ("the low sun makes the colour" [G, 641–643; LE, 134]). Vivien mocks the Queen's adultery by addressing her, "O Heaven's own white / Earth-angel" (MV, 79–80), the inverted stress falling heavily on earth. Guinevere herself rationalizes her adultery by asking, "But who can gaze upon the Sun in Heaven?" and demanding of her lover "a touch of earth" (LE, 123, 133).

For the possible influence of G. S. Faber's The Origin of Pagan Idolatry (1816) on Tennyson's conception of Arthur as a sun-god, see W. D. Paden, Tennyson in Egypt: A Study of the Imagery in His Earlier Work (Lawrence, Kans., University of Kansas Press, 1942), pp. 78–85, and Valerie Pitt, Tennyson Laureate (London, Barrie and Rockliff, 1962), pp. 214, 275.

Star, Noonday Sun, Evening Star, and Death, who symbolize
in miniature the larger movement of the *Idylls* through the
four seasons. The opening idylls are as bathed in light as
the later idylls are shrouded in darkness. Gareth first sees
Camelot in the early morning of a spring day, the middle
idylls take place in the high noon of summer, and the
autumnal "Last Tournament" marks the transition to the
winter's night of "Guinevere" and "The Passing of Arthur."
With the waning of Arthur's power, the sun itself is eclipsed
from the poem. The word *sun* occurs more than five times
as frequently in the first three idylls as in the last three.
And all but one of the later references are to the setting sun
or contrast the young king at the height of his power with
the older king in his decline. The single exception is the
closing line of the poem, which describes the dawn of the new
year and suggests the eternal recurrence of the cycle of
growth and decay to which Arthur is joined in "The
Coming." [9]

Throughout "The Coming of Arthur" the past is absorbed
into the present and is prophetic of the future. Certain key
events predate the presumed "present" of the idyll: the
birth of Arthur and his arming with Excalibur, the internecine
wars of the kings who preceded Arthur, the clearing of the
primordial wilderness. Other events have occurred in the
immediate past and are narrated directly by the omniscient
speaker: Arthur's sending of Lancelot in "latter April" to
to fetch Guinevere, their arrival "among the flowers in May,"
the wedding and coronation. Still others lie in the immediate
future: the wars against Rome, the conquest of the rebellious
princes, the consolidation of the realm. Although still the
young king of a freshly-founded kingdom, Arthur takes on
a certain borrowed venerability from the long-established
rites of his marriage and from the curiously involuted
accounts of his birth. Leodogran, Guinevere's father, in
trying to ascertain Arthur's legitimacy, questions his "hoary
chamberlain," who in turn refers him to Merlin and Bleys,

both twice as old as the aged chamberlain. Bellicent carries
the narrative into even further reaches of the past, although
the mystery can be no older than Bellicent herself, Arthur's
elder half-sister. As she discusses these "secret things"
(317) with Leodogran, her young sons pass by, and in six
lines of utmost economy Tennyson introduces two important
characters and glances ahead to the end of the *Idylls:*

> And Gawain went, and breaking into song
> Sprang out, and followed by his flying hair
> Ran like a colt, and leapt at all he saw:
> But Modred laid his ear beside the doors,
> And there half-heard; the same that afterward
> Struck for the throne, and striking found his doom.
>   (319–324)

Gawain, ever paralleling the seasons of the realm, is seen
here in his early spring, with a hint of the animal impetuosity
("leapt at all he saw") that will later earn him the title
"light of love" (PE, 353). Modred is ever Modred, never
young, never old, always the subtle beast poised to strike.

Despite the fluidity of time in "The Coming of Arthur,"
the reader is never disoriented; instead he observes Arthur
imposing order upon temporal as well as political chaos.
The order is built into the very syntax of the lines, with
their balanced repetitions and parallel clauses. In the Last
Battle the reverse occurs; the confused slaughter, the shrieks,
the clashings, the "formless fear" are reflected in the
syntactical confusion, and the virtual absence of verbs fuses
the separate actions into a simultaneous phantasmagoria.
In "The Coming of Arthur," however, the closing paragraph
repeats the opening, drawing a verbal circle around the
"space" of Arthur's reign; the sequence of parallel verbs
(drew . . . fought . . . overcame), the alliterating "made a
realm and reigned," the biblical deliberateness of the repeated
and's all quicken our sense that we have witnessed a new
Genesis, that Arthur has made a cosmos out of chaos:

And Arthur and his knighthood for a space
Were all one will, and through that strength the King
Drew in the petty princedoms under him,
Fought, and in twelve great battles overcame
The heathen hordes, and made a realm and reigned.
                                                    (514–518)

Time, whose movements seem so vast in "The Coming of
Arthur," all but stops in "Gareth and Lynette." We are still
in the bright spring of the reign and Arthur remains young.
Yet he has already "swept the dust of ruined Rome / From
off the threshold of the realm" (133–134), and Gawain is
now a proven knight (27). And although we learn in "The
Last Tournament" that Tristram "came late" and swore
"but by the shell" (269–270), he has already been knighted.
The mention of Tristram and the far more sinister
appearance at court of a messenger from Mark introduce
the only chill notes in the idyll, and with them a sudden rush
of time. But for the balance of "Gareth and Lynette" all is
harmony and blossoming:

                    The birds made
Melody on branch, and melody in mid air.
The damp hill-slopes were quickened into green,
And the live green had kindled into flowers,
For it was past the time of Easterday.
                                                    (179–183)

The leisurely pace of the narrative suggests there is world
enough and time even for recalcitrant lovers like Lynette.
Freed of nature's laws, time moves not at all or in reverse; a
monstrous mutation like the aged Knight of Death—"A huge
man-beast of boundless savagery" (622)—turns out to be
a blooming boy.

Of all the idylls, "Gareth and Lynette" deals most directly
with the theme of illusion and reality. The supreme illusion
in this most "timeless" of the idylls is chronological time.
As Gareth approaches the distant Camelot, he sees a city

which, having grown up about Arthur, is necessarily of indeterminate age, for like Arthur it exists in time and transcends time and shares with him an equivocal reality. The disguised Gareth gazes on a city which is itself disguised in a veil of mist:

> Far off they saw the silver-misty morn
> Rolling her smoke about the Royal mount,
> That rose between the forest and the field.
> At times the summit of the high city flashed;
> At times the spires and turrets half-way down
> Pricked through the mist; at times the great gate shone
> Only, that opened on the field below:
> Anon, the whole fair city had disappeared.
>
> (186–193)

One of Gareth's retinue cautions that they go no further, for "here is a city of Enchanters" (196), which of course it is, having been built by the magician Merlin in league with "enchanters" such as Tennyson. The city is enchanted in another sense, for, according to Merlin, it houses men enthralled

> by such vows, as is a shame
> A man should not be bound by, yet the which
> No man can keep.
>
> (266–268)

Yet at this stage of the realm, the city, like the vows on which it is founded, appears to be the reality and the barbarous past is the illusion. Hence Gareth can silence the fears of his men with mere laughter; his own romantic idealism half brings Camelot into being, just as Camelot endows him with an identity. Although of royal blood, Gareth enters the city as a nameless peasant: "Let be my name until I make my name! / My deeds will speak" (562–563). They do, and for a space refute the lingering doubts of his companion:

Lord, there is no such city anywhere,
But all a vision . . .

(203–204)

Like everything else in "Gareth and Lynette," the lines are
not quite what they seem. *Vision* we take to mean *illusion*,
and the city's vanishing in the mist, together with Merlin's
critique of the vows, gives full weight to this meaning.
But *vision* also bears a contrary sense—"the heavens were
opened, and I saw visions of God" (Ezek. 1:1)—and in this
sense the mists symbolize the illusions of men in nature;
Gareth's skeptical companion sees Camelot through a glass
darkly, for the city behind the mist is the ultimate reality.
This second meaning becomes dominant as Gareth passes
through the gate of Camelot and sees carved on its sides the
"sacred fish" and weirdly intricate sculptures of Arthur's
wars:

New things and old co-twisted, as if Time
Were nothing, so inveterately, that men
Were giddy gazing there . . .

(222–224)

Although the realm is recently founded, the frieze of Arthur's
battles and the emblems of his majesty are "worn with wind
and storm" (218). As Gareth stares at the luxuriantly
intertwined figures, they seem to writhe and curl as if alive
(227–231). All times are co-present in Camelot, and Gareth's
giddiness stems from this disorienting fusion. Tennyson's
paradoxical epithet for Camelot—"the dim rich city" (LE,
840, 842)—expresses this synthesis of obscurity and opulence,
of the dim past that is richly alive in the city's present.
Percivale later speaks of the "dim rich city" (HG, 228)
of Camelot,

Built by old kings, age after age, so old
The King himself had fears that it would fall,
So strange, and rich, and dim . . .

(HG, 340–342)

Camelot seems to predate Arthur, yet Arthur's "date" is itself uncertain, and the whole point of the ideals embodied in both is their timelessness. Because those ideals can never be fully realized and their efficacy is subject to doubt, they remain "dim"; because they epitomize the highest human aspirations of past and future, they are "rich." Parts of Camelot are already crumbling, like accretions from former ages that have outlived their use. Parts have yet to be built; of the twelve great windows in Arthur's hall, one remains blank, "and who shall blazon it? when and how?" (HG, 254).

Although the dim rich city draws together all these meanings, the dominant image of Camelot throughout the *Idylls* is musical rather than visual. The melody on branch and in mid air that Gareth hears before entering Camelot is a lyric preparation for the great peal of music that greets him at the city gates. The first melody is the exquisite sensuous music of the dying generations caught up in the cycle of nature; the second is supersensuous and stops Gareth in his tracks:

> For an ye heard a music, like enow
> They are building still, seeing the city is built
> To music, therefore never built at all,
> And therefore built for ever.
>
> (271–274)

Tennyson draws on the myth, as old as cities themselves, of the city as a sacred center, an *axis mundi* where heaven and earth intersect. The "sacred mount of Camelot" (HG, 227) is just such a center, supernatural in origin and supertemporal in duration. Like Troy, which was founded to the music of Apollo's lyre, or Thebes, founded to the music of Amphion, Camelot is "built to music."[10] But since in St. Paul's phrase we can have "no continuing city" on earth (Hebrews 13:14), Camelot is "never built," although the ideal that animates it predates its founding and will survive its fall, and hence the city is "built forever."

The Geraint idylls fall midway in time and tone between
the fairy tale of "Gareth and Lynette" and the tragedy of
"Balin and Balan." A rumor (not yet confirmed) has already
arisen concerning Lancelot and the Queen, and Geraint,
fearing that the "taint" will touch his wife, takes her from
Camelot. One detects in the action and setting of the Geraint
idylls the first consequences of the falling away from the
vows. The rumored infidelity prompts Geraint to lie to the
King and leave the civility of the court on the pretext that
he must purge his territories of marauding bandits. The
pretext proves to be an imperative necessity; the wilderness
that Geraint and Enid enter is as treacherous as the desolate
wastes of "The Coming of Arthur," for it is inhabited by
men who have lapsed back into beasts—the brutal Earl
Doorm, his savage spearmen, and the wild Limours, "half
ridden off with by the thing he rode" (GE, 460). The
mock-jousts in "Gareth and Lynette" prove mortal in
"Geraint and Enid." Geraint drives his spear through the
breast of a bandit, stripping off his armor like a man "that
skins the wild beast after slaying him" (GE, 93). And in a
gory inversion of Gareth's harmless cleaving of the helmet of
the Knight of Death, Geraint in one blow beheads
Earl Doorm.

The brutality in "Geraint and Enid" anticipates the later
idylls, while its Cinderella story of the rescued princess-
in-rags harks back to the romance of "Gareth and Lynette."
The two elements tug uneasily at one another, and both the
"Marriage of Geraint" and "Geraint and Enid" are clouded
by the murkiness of unreconciled intentions. These least
successful of the idylls are perhaps necessarily so, for just as
they straddle two genres, so they mark that uncertain period
in the realm when fidelity still has its rewards—the
Griselda-like endurance of Enid wins back the errant
Geraint—but infidelity has exacted its first chilling
consequences. The Round Table can still exert a regenerative
influence, converting Edyrn from a career of crime to one of

service, as it soon fails to do for Balin. But the outlying
districts of the kingdom have already become a "common
sewer" (MG, 39) and require that Arthur once again "till
the wastes," clear the "dark places and let in the law"
(GE, 941–942). At this stage in the *Idylls*, however, the
victory clearly belongs to Arthur, Geraint's doubts of his wife
prove groundless, and in an ending incongruously
reminiscent of Tennyson's domestic idylls, the fruitful
"Enid the Good" gives birth to "Enids and Geraints / Of
times to be" (GE, 964–965).

This last of the idylls to end happily marks the end of the
first large movement of the poem. "Balin and Balan" takes
place not long after "Geraint and Enid," about midway
through the calendar of the reign. The opening lines imply
sufficient passage of time since the founding for the tributary
princes to have grown lax "of late" in their fealty. The
temporal texture of the poem is enriched with recurrent
reminiscences, such as Guinevere's of the fair days when
Lancelot brought her to Camelot. Arthur is now in full
maturity ("The light-winged spirit of his youth returned"),
and the banners commemorating his twelve great battles "stir,
as they stirred of old" (86). For the lately-arrived Balin,
the battles have acquired the half-legendary status of heroic
echoes from a still-fresh past.

At the start of "Balin and Balan" we feel both renewal and
loss, as is appropriate to the joyous moment of Balin's
rejoining the Round Table and to the calamity that lies ahead.
"Balin and Balan" repeats in miniature the larger movement
of the *Idylls*, from the lyricism of its beginning to the bestial
discord of its close. The landscape expresses this duality.
At the start,

> when Sir Balin entered hall,
> The Lost one Found was greeted as in Heaven*

---

* Tennyson alludes to the parables of the lost sheep ("Rejoice with
me; for I have found my sheep which was lost") and of the prodigal son

With joy that blazed itself in woodland wealth
Of leaf, and gayest garlandage of flowers.
(77–80)

But after his mad flight from the Queen's garden, he enters the tangled, "skyless" forest and dwells as a "savage among the savage woods" (479).

Woods are always perilous in the *Idylls*, and in the "wild woods of Broceliande" (MV, 2) the realm suffers its first capital loss in the person of Merlin. Balin's "violences" are the product of a personal pathology; Merlin's "great melancholy" (MV, 187) is culturally induced. As a seer, he foreknows the collapse of the realm and is made impotent by his own prophetic prowess. He is the first to feel the world-weariness that soon afflicts Lancelot and Tristram and that marks all of the later idylls. That weariness is in part due to his own great age, in part to the age of the kingdom. At the time of the founding, Merlin has already seen a "hundred winters" (CA, 280); but the figure only hints at his true antiquity. The charm that Vivien wrests from him is recorded in a book whose language

has long gone by.
So long, that mountains have arisen since
With cities on their flanks . . .
(MV, 672–674)

"Less old . . . yet older" (MV, 554) than the Eastern king for whom the book was written, Merlin is essentially ageless. He has built Arthur's "havens, ships, and halls" (MV, 166); his wisdom goes back to the pagan past, which he has placed in the service of the Arthurian present. His fall

("be glad: for this thy brother was dead, and is alive again; and was lost, and is found") in Luke 15. The parable of the prodigal son is especially apt in its portrayal of two brothers of opposite nature, and both parables underscore the tragedy of Balin, who although lost and then found amidst rejoicing, is in the end lost irretrievably.

breaks the kingdom's link to that past, and with it the bridge
to futurity. Even more than the King, Merlin invests the
Idylls with an aura of preternatural antiquity. But unlike
Arthur, he is magical rather than supernatural, and it is
time-in-nature whose horizons he extends. Merlin is neither
born nor dies during the time of the poem; with a fine
equivocation, Tennyson leaves him lying "*as* dead" (967) in
the hollow oak. Yet his blood, as he tells Vivien, "hath
earnest in it of far springs to be" (555).

Vivien arrives at court at what seems to be the Golden Age
of the kingdom,

> While all the heathen lay at Arthur's feet,
> And no quest came, but all was joust and play.
> (MV, 142–143)

The external enemy has been vanquished and the realm is
now exposed to the more divisive perils of peace. And so
Mark dispatches Vivien on a mission of internal subversion
which she undertakes like a

> little rat that borest in the dyke
> Thy hole by night to let the boundless deep
> Down upon far-off cities while they dance.
> (MV, 110–112)

The sultry, oppressive atmosphere of "Merlin and Vivien,"
with its threat of impending storm, reflects both Merlin's
mood and the explosive passions underlying this long hot
summer of the realm. Knowing that he has outlived his
usefulness, Merlin is the more helpless to resist Vivien's
advances. If so great a fall seems premature, it has its ironic
appropriateness. For Merlin's constant theme has been the
difference between the apparent and the real, and he has
perceived what Arthur has not: the outward flourishing of the
kingdom masks an inner decay. The curve of its political
power is still in the ascendant but its moral cohesion has long

been waning. The gap between the two accounts for an apparent imbalance in the symbolic season. Seven of the idylls—from "The Marriage of Geraint" through "Pelleas and Ettarre"—are concentrated in the summer, but they increasingly accentuate the blight overtly manifested in "The Last Tournament." The protracted summer underscores the brevity of the later idylls, and Tennyson's description of the symbolic season corresponds to our experience of the poem: " 'The Coming of Arthur' is on the night of the New Year; when he is wedded 'the world is white with May'; on a summer night the vision of the Holy Grail appears; and the 'Last Tournament' is in the 'yellowing autumn-tide.' Guinevere flees thro' the mists of autumn, and Arthur's death takes place at midnight in midwinter." [11]

"Lancelot and Elaine" takes place in the high summer of the realm. The luxuriance of the season reflects itself in the luxuriance of the verse: Guinevere's oriel window stands open to the heat, and as she flings Lancelot's gift of diamonds through the vine-clad casement,

> down they flashed, and smote the stream.
> Then from the smitten surface flashed, as it were,
> Diamonds to meet them . . .
> (1227–1229)

Elaine is buried with "gorgeous obsequies," and the Tournament of Diamonds takes place in a meadow as richly colored as the plumed knights or the "peopled gallery which half round / Lay like a rainbow fallen upon the grass" (428–429). These are the last great spectacles of the realm. In "The Last Tournament" the pageantry is drowned in autumn rains, and in place of the ceremonial funeral of Elaine, Mark butchers his cousin Tristram in the dark.

The murder of kin is one of the darker motifs linking the separate idylls. The motif figures prominently in a scene at the start of "Lancelot and Elaine" that also defines the calendar of the reign more precisely than any other passage in the *Idylls*. Long before his coronation Arthur had wandered through a gloomy tarn where two brothers had slain each other, their corpses lying untouched "till all their bones were bleached, / And lichened into colour with the crags" (43–44). One brother had been a king and still bore a crown of nine diamonds when Arthur, unaware, trod over

> that crowned skeleton, and the skull
> Brake from the nape, and from the skull the crown
> Rolled into light, and turning on its rims
> Fled like a glittering rivulet to the tarn:
> And down the shingly scaur he plunged, and caught,
> And set it on his head, and in his heart
> Heard murmurs, "Lo, thou likewise shalt be King."
> (49–55)

The primeval glen of the dead kings recalls the wastes of "The Coming of Arthur," where Urien attacks Leodogran, "his brother king" (35). Both scenes reenact the archetypal fratricide in the *Idylls*, Balin and Balan, and all three point to the Last Battle, when Arthur will preside as king of the dead over his fallen knights, slaying and in turn slain by his nephew Modred.*

While the finding of the diamonds occurs before the founding of the Round Table and prefigures its fall, it also places the main action of "Lancelot and Elaine" in or very near the tenth year of the reign. Soon after his coronation

---

* In Malory, Modred is Arthur's son, conceived in incestuous union with his half-sister. Arthur's fall is explicitly attributed to his sin, although the sin is mitigated by his not recognizing his sister as such at the time of the incest. In the *Idylls* Tennyson denies any suggestion that Modred is Arthur's son and in successive revisions casts doubt on *any* consanguinity between the two, although he never fully suppresses a possible connection. He comes closest to complete denial in "Guinevere," where Arthur refers to Modred as "the man they call / My sister's son—no kin of mine" (569–570). But he lets stand Bellicent's ambiguous answer to Leodogran's question whether or not Bellicent, the mother of Modred, is Arthur's sister: "These be secret

Arthur institutes the annual Diamond Tournament, and in each of the previous eight jousts Lancelot has gained the prize, the final tournament taking place in "Lancelot and Elaine." A ten-year interval between the founding and the "present" is further suggested by Elaine's reading a "pretty history to herself" in the scars on Lancelot's armor: "this cut is fresh; / That ten years back; this dealt him at Caerlyle" (18–22).[12] Such calculations are scarcely ambrosia for the imagination, but they enable us to state with reasonable exactitude what any reader of the *Idylls* must feel: the later idylls are not only less leisurely in narration and notably briefer than the earlier,[13] but they are crowded into an ever-foreshortening time-scale. The first seven idylls, through "Lancelot and Elaine," are spread over the first ten years of the reign; the last five idylls are compressed into two years, and of these, four take place within the final year. As Arthur's impending doom comes ever closer, the symbolic season advances with dramatic suddenness, in consonance with our actual experience of shortening days and lengthening nights as the year approaches its end.

We can have no experience of time without recurrence, yet recurrence, while it deepens the sense of time, also serves to foreshorten the interval between recurrences. The repeated patterns throughout the *Idylls* have the same dual effect of enriching and compressing time. They constitute a kind of built-in memory or echo chamber which becomes more and more resonant as the poem progresses, so that Arthur's

---

things" (CA, 317). Arthur's disclaimer of kinship may be taken as a literal denial that Bellicent is his half-sister, or as a figurative assertion that kinship is more than a matter of blood and that he bears no conceivable moral connection to the bestial Modred. By straddling the question of the King's blood relation to Modred (or, for that matter, to any other character in the poem), Tennyson keeps open the possibility of Arthur's supernatural origins. Also, by expunging the incestuous taint from his "blameless king," Tennyson shifts the cause of Arthur's fall from the accident of unwitting incest to the wider issue of the erosion of human trust under the stress of time.

reign seems to endure not for a dozen years but through a whole cycle of civilization. Yet the young Arthur's foreseeing his own death as he crowns himself with the dead king's crown—"Lo, thou likewise shalt be King"—compresses the whole reign into a single continuous moment.

Although Arthur ages in the course of the poem, he wears his years like a borrowed mask to be cast off at death, when he reenters his true temporal medium, eternity. Merlin possesses great but static antiquity; from the start he has reached the outer limit of age in nature and never alters. Lancelot above all others in the *Idylls* bears the burden of *passing* time. In this he is the opposite of Gawain, who also ages but offers so little resistance to the temporal medium through which he moves that age seems never to touch him. Lancelot aspires to live and move and have his being in Arthur's time yet is entrapped in natural time, and it is this "war of Time against the soul of man" (GL, 1168) which mars him prematurely.

We see the first scars of that struggle in "Merlin and Vivien," when Vivien on entering the court wonders, "Is that the Lancelot? goodly—ay, but gaunt" (101). Lancelot is further aged in "Lancelot and Elaine" by contrast with the youthful Elaine, who nurses his wounds as he lies "unsleek, unshorn, / Gaunt as it were the skeleton of himself" (810–811). Once we are told that Lancelot is "more than twice" her years, and once with perhaps a touch of hyperbole he chivalrously urges her not to yield herself to a man thrice her age (256, 948). Renouncing the love of the innocent Elaine, he turns back in guilty loyalty to Guinevere, for whom, as for Lancelot, their love is now a remembered rapture heavy with the sense of present pain. The stately Guinevere of the earlier idylls moves "languidly" (84) through "Lancelot and Elaine," and the troubled Lancelot looks "in half disdain / At love, life, all things" (1230–1231).

This temper of despair first seen in Merlin and then in Lancelot and Guinevere has become a general disease of the will in "The Holy Grail." The court has fallen on decadent days, and a kind of spiritual sensation-seeking replaces the waning ethic of chivalric service to the King and to one's lady. Elaine's death in quest of love had been a personal tragedy softened by the ritual splendors of her waterborne funeral. The knights' quest for the Grail proves equally fatal, but the disaster is social as well as individual. The wasteland of sand and thorn through which the knights "follow wandering fires" (319) symbolizes the spiritual infertility of the realm, and the half-ruined Camelot to which only a remnant returns has already begun to lapse back into the wilderness.

The passage of calendar time only in part accounts for the sense of general ruin. Although the quest for the Grail takes place not long after Elaine's death and lasts only a year, by narrating the action indirectly and in the past Tennyson invests it with an almost legendary remoteness. Most of "The Holy Grail" consists of the dramatic monologue of Percivale; but unlike the classic examples of the form in Browning, where the present tense accounts for much of the immediacy, "The Holy Grail" is twice removed from the present. In the introductory paragraph we learn that after the Grail quest Percivale had become a monk in a distant abbey "and not long after, died." As we overhear the posthumous voice of Percivale the present seems visibly to recede before our eyes, and the ghostly heaps of stone which greet the returning knights appear even more ruinous, for the narrator who describes them is now himself a ghost.

These narrative devices, together with such signs of time as Percivale's reference to the mighty hall which Merlin built "long ago" (226), make Camelot's decline seem part of the natural passing of the old order. The same effect is achieved through the progressive aging of the characters. Lancelot, for example, is rumored to be the father of Galahad, who, though still young, has already been knighted (138–145). Throughout "The Holy Grail," however, cyclic time is

subordinate to apocalyptic time, as symbolized by the sudden
tempest that bursts over Camelot, sheers the statuary off
Arthur's hall, and figures in each of the knights' visions of
the Grail. Arthur is ominously absent from Camelot when
the knights vow to seek the Grail, but he sees the lightning
break over the distant city and rushes back

> In horror lest the work by Merlin wrought,
> Dreamlike, should on the sudden vanish, wrapt
> In unremorseful folds of rolling fire.
>
> (259–261)

The fiery end of Camelot has been foreseen from the
beginning, and Arthur's fears for his dreamlike city recall
the apprehensions of Gareth that Camelot may vanish in the
mist. Percivale and Galahad traverse a Dantesque landscape
lit by the same apocalyptic flames that strike at Camelot:

> And Galahad fled along . . . bridge by bridge,
> And every bridge as quickly as he crost
> Sprang into fire and vanished, though I yearned
> To follow; and thrice above him all the heavens
> Opened and blazed with thunder such as seemed
> Shoutings of all the sons of God.
>
> (504–509)

Lancelot rides wildly along a sterile shore and, driven mad
by guilt, describes the storm as a kind of Last Judgment,
complete with trumpet blast:

> then I came
> All in my folly to the naked shore,
> Wide flats, where nothing but coarse grasses grew;
> But such a blast, my King, began to blow,
> So loud a blast along the shore and sea,
> Ye could not hear the waters for the blast,
> Though heapt in mounds and ridges all the sea
> Drove like a cataract, and all the sand
> Swept like a river, and the clouded heavens
> Were shaken with the motion and the sound.
>
> (789–798)

The tempest originates in nature yet seems to come from beyond it and strike the realm with the force of a supernatural judgment. As at Arthur's birth and death, the boundaries of earth and heaven are obscured; night turns into day, day into night, and time and season are wrenched out of their natural course. This transection of the temporal and eternal is most pronounced in "The Coming of Arthur," "The Passing of Arthur," and "The Holy Grail," and in all three is accompanied by violent disorder in man and nature. Of all the Round Table idylls, "The Holy Grail" thus bears a uniquely close relation to the two frame poems. It marks the end of an epoch, the transition from aspiration to desperation.

The four remaining idylls are tightly linked in time and subject, the end of each leading immediately to the next. At the close of "Pelleas and Ettarre" the maddened Pelleas vows to become the enemy of the Round Table; at the start of "The Last Tournament" he reappears in the guise of the Red Knight, who has founded a kind of anti-Camelot in the North dedicated to the destruction of Arthur's realm. Arthur returns to Camelot at the close of "The Last Tournament" to be greeted by the sobs of the Fool and to find the Queen's bower dark and deserted. "Guinevere" opens with the Queen weeping at Almesbury and alone with the novice, on a night

> Blurred by the creeping mist, for all abroad,
> Beneath a moon unseen albeit at full,
> The white mist, like a face-cloth to the face,
> Clung to the dead earth, and the land was still.

After the final meeting of Arthur and Guinevere, the King rides off into the rolling fog, until he becomes "as mist / Before her, moving ghostlike to his doom" (600–601). The "death-white mist" at the end of "Guinevere" enshrouds the field of the Last Battle, to which Arthur leads his troops immediately upon leaving Almesbury. The four idylls form a single swift movement accentuated by the sudden rapidity of the seasonal changes. In "Pelleas and Ettarre" it is still high summer; the field in which Pelleas first sees Ettarre shimmers with heat, and the nights are warm enough for Pelleas to discover his lady sleeping outdoors with Gawain in a garden of red and white roses, symbolic transplants from Guinevere's garden, but now with "brambles mixt / And overgrowing them" (413–414). "The Last Tournament" takes place "all in a death-dumb autumn-dripping gloom" (750), and Arthur dies on the midnight of the winter solstice.

Pelleas is the last of the recruits to the Round Table, knighted along with others "from the four winds" (PE, 141) to fill the gap left by the Grail quest. Arthur's world is changing, widening, coming loose at the seams. A full generation now separates those who took the vows at the founding from those who compete with Pelleas in the Tournament of Youth. The title ironically emphasizes the passage of time as does the recipient of the prize, the much-handled and overripe Ettarre, who receives from Pelleas the suggestive sword and golden circlet. Pelleas' quest for the carnal Ettarre is as disillusioning as the knights' quest for the Grail; after his betrayal, his passion for possession becomes a passion for destruction, until in attacking Arthur he destroys himself. As a latter-day Gareth, Pelleas too has visions, but they are the visions of a youth whose world has suddenly been shattered. In a scene of extraordinary ferocity, he rides down a crippled beggar, and, glancing back at Camelot, sees not a fair city of spires but

High up in heaven the hall that Merlin built,
Blackening against the dead-green stripes of even,
"Black nest of rats," he groaned, "ye build too high."
(542–544)

All of Pelleas' actions after his apostasy from the Round Table are still conditioned by the values of the Round Table.

His kingship over the bestial knights of the North bears
the same inverted connection to Arthur's rule as a black mass
does to the sacred liturgy, except that the original text, as
it were, has become so corrupt that the parody is now the
reality. Tristram represents a far greater break with the past
than does Pelleas. Instead of attacking Arthur's order, he
steps wholly outside it. This departure is marked in the
symbolic season by the sudden shift from the summer idylls
to the ruinously autumnal "Last Tournament." Pelleas came
late but took the vows in dead earnest. Tristram, though
knighted earlier, came after the heathen wars were over and
swore "but by the shell" (269–270). Like Isolt, he is without
illusions and incapable of guilt. The two sets of adulterous
lovers in "The Last Tournament"—Lancelot and Guinevere,
Tristram and Isolt—were born into different worlds and
suffer very different sorrows; the one pair is agonized by its
own lies and the other is in despair at having no lies to
believe in. "Lie to me," Isolt begs Tristram; "I should suck /
Lies like sweet wines" (639–640). Nothing in the *Idylls*
more poignantly marks the passage of time than the scene in
which these modern lovers, seeking "new life, new love, to
suit the newer day" (279), seem immemorially weary,
willfully free of Arthur's constraints yet impotent in their
freedom.

Even while condemning Arthur's vows as a momentary
madness, Tristram paints a picture of the King that makes
credible his initial assent, when he first beheld

> That victor of the Pagan throned in hall—
> His hair, a sun that rayed from off a brow
> Like hillsnow high in heaven, the steel-blue eyes,
> The golden beard that clothed his lips with light—
>   . . . he seemed to me no man,
> But Michaël trampling Satan; so I sware,
> Being amazed.
>   (660–663, 667–669)

In a similar juxtaposition of the dark present and bright
past, Guinevere at Almesbury recalls the "golden days"
before their sin, when Lancelot brought her to Camelot and
they

> Rode under groves that looked a paradise
> Of blossoms, over sheets of hyacinth
> That seemed the heavens upbreaking through the earth.
> (G, 386–388)

Arthur breaks in upon her reverie to denounce her adultery
as the root of all the betrayals that have now made Lancelot
his enemy and raised civil war in the realm. In the midst
of this hardest of all Arthur's sayings, he forces Guinevere
to recall the magnificence of the achievement she has
wrecked, the soiling of the vows, the ruin of the Round Table,

> A glorious company, the flower of men,
> To serve as model for the mighty world,
> And be the fair beginning of a time.
> (G, 461–463)

As the realm sinks further and further into the abyss, it
reemerges in retrospective glory. Tennyson's most daring
use of retrospect for this purpose occurs in the narrative of
the naive young nun who keeps vigil with Guinevere before
Arthur's arrival. Unaware of the Queen's identity, she
speaks of the signs and wonders that years ago accompanied
the founding of the Round Table, "before the coming of the
sinful Queen" (G, 268). Her father, now dead, had been
one of Arthur's knights, and her account of his recollections,
although dating back only a generation, takes on the aura
of a garbled legend barely recoverable from the past. The
mystery of the King's birth, invested with the highest powers
of Tennyson's imagination in "The Coming of Arthur," is
here lowered in key to a folk tale. Refracted through the
mind of the novice, divinity has already shaded off into

superstition, and the city built to music is a fairy palace with magical spigots gushing wine. As Guinevere hears herself described as the wicked Queen in league with the "evil work" of Lancelot, she turns to the novice and asks,

> "O closed about by narrowing nunnery-walls,
> What knowest thou of the world, and all its lights
> And shadows, all the wealth and all the woe?"
>
> (G, 340–342)

The whole weight of Guinevere's moral experience is compressed into her question. The sinful Queen assumes an undeniable grandeur as we observe her observing herself in the distorting mirror of the nun's simplisms. The scene has the uncanny effect of inducing the reader to defend the reality and integrity of Tennyson's fictional Guinevere against the distortions of Tennyson's fictional nun. The nun's fantastic account of the wonders of Arthur's coming also serves, by contrast, to authenticate the "original" wonders, themselves of course no less fictional.

Tennyson's incorporation of these naive fictions into the immeasurably more sophisticated fiction of the *Idylls* breaks down our conventional distinctions between the illusory and the real. In the same way, our habitual notions of time undergo a progressive disorientation. As the founding recedes further and further into the past, we become more and more conscious of it in a continuous present, so that Camelot is still being built in our mind's eye as it goes up in flames, just as those flames were present in our imagination even as the city was being built. In some ultimate sense that only the experience of the poem can convey, nothing ever happens only once and everything that happens, happens simultaneously with its opposite. Camelot and the wasteland, music and discord, vows and betrayals, white roses and red, men imitating God and lapsing into beasts, growth and decay, soul and sense, reality and illusion, time and eternity

—the whole dialectic of interlocked opposites is held in
dynamic equilibrium and the opposites themselves, as
Tennyson constantly suggests, are fractured halves of the
same identity. Arthur's coming is shadowed with the
foreknowledge of his passing, but his passing contains the
possibility of a second coming. In this Arthur imitates the
course of the symbolic season, which as it revolves toward
winter is also approaching spring. Lancelot and Guinevere
are marred and marked by their sin, and grow in grace because
of it. The ruins of Camelot recall the city in its initial
splendor, its fall persuading us of its prior reality. These
reciprocal movements of rise and fall are held in perfect poise
throughout the *Idylls*. In the beginning we are primarily
aware of ascent and at the end, of decline. But both are
constantly present, like the recurring pairs of symbols that
accompany them. Prophecy heightens the sense of impending
fall when the rising curve is dominant; retrospect
accentuates the former ascendancy when the falling curve
is dominant. As the rush toward doom threatens to become
too precipitous, the *Idylls* seems to give birth to a second
myth, a former glory validated in disaster:

> Such times have been not since the light that led
> The holy Elders with the gift of myrrh.
> But now the whole Round Table is dissolved
> Which was an image of the mighty world,
> And I, the last, go forth companionless,
> And the days darken round me . . .
>
> (PA, 400–405)

IV · Landscape

On the eve of the Last Battle, Arthur looks back upon the defeat of all his purposes and laments that the world seems to have been made by some lesser god who "had not force to shape it as he would" (PA, 15). Throughout the *Idylls* nature, mirroring man, is at war with itself, ever aspiring to some higher order and ever lapsing into the primal chaos. Like the moral wilderness, the physical wilderness constantly encroaches on the space that Arthur has cleared. The obscure powers of the North are both renegade knights from Arthur's court and aboriginal forces within nature, ever poised to fill the vacuum created by the withdrawal of the King's power. The Manichean struggle between powers of light and darkness, order and disorder, humanity and bestiality, is internalized within the characters and also projected upon the landscapes through which they move. Tangled thickets and orderly gardens, sultry meadows and violent tempests are all extensions of human consciousness, a kind of natural amphitheater in which the moral drama of the poem is enacted.

Tennyson deliberately blurs the distinction between character and setting, just as he blurs the boundaries separating past, present, and future. Despite the thousands of lines of natural description throughout Tennyson's poetry, he is least of all what he is most commonly assumed to be

—a purely descriptive poet. There are no "descriptive backgrounds" in the *Idylls*, only foregrounds in which we are at times primarily conscious of a particular character, at times of a particular setting.* At first glance this seems like a fancy way of saying there is a good deal of "pathetic fallacy" in the *Idylls*, which of course there is, provided one understands by the term a more than merely fanciful coloring of nature in the light of human emotion. The symbolic season which flowers and fades along with Arthur is probably the most sustained pathetic fallacy in our literature. Some such latent animism is present in all natural description, however sophisticated, and it is so current in our daily speech that we use it unconsciously, as in speaking of threatening weather or calm seas. Yet much of what is commonly dismissed as pathetic fallacy is in fact something quite different. The phrase carries an unfortunate connotation, implying the primary reality of the human subject, whose emotion is "fallaciously" projected upon the external order of nature. In the *Idylls*, however, character is as much an extension of landscape as landscape is of character. In this sense the symbolic season does not imitate Arthur's declining career but Arthur's career imitates the course of the seasons, in whose cycle, as a dying god, he is tragically enmeshed.

Tennyson uses landscape, then, not as a decorative adjunct to character but as the mythopoeic soil in which character

---

* In a review of Tennyson's early poems, John Stuart Mill noted the conspicuous absence of that "rather vapid species of composition usually termed descriptive poetry—for there is not in these volumes one passage of pure description: but the power of *creating* scenery, in keeping with some state of human feeling; so fitted to it as to be the embodied symbol of it, and to summon up the state of feeling itself, with a force not to be surpassed by anything but reality." (Reprinted from the *London Review* of July 1835 in John Jump, ed., *Tennyson: The Critical Heritage* [London, Routledge & Kegan Paul], p. 86.) Mill's phrasing is strikingly reminiscent of the review that Arthur Hallam published of the same volume four years earlier and that Mill perhaps unconsciously recalled in writing his own review. See Hallam's criticism of *Poems, Chiefly Lyrical* cited on p. 26 above.

is rooted and takes its being. George Santayana has analyzed this use of landscape in an essay in which he defends the pathetic fallacy as the means of recovering the primitive, natural symbolism inherent in all great poetry. Character divorced from its environing landscape, Santayana argues, represents only a "fragmentary unity," for "characters are initially embedded in life, as the gods themselves are originally embedded in Nature." Through landscape the poet restores the "natural confusion" of inner and outer worlds common to ancient modes of experience before the classifying intelligence assigned them to separate spheres. Landscape recalls and consecrates this half-forgotten unity.[1]

   Throughout his life Tennyson could summon to consciousness that strangely animistic sense of nature we associate with our own individual childhood and with the childhood of the race. One of his earliest memories was of outspreading his arms in a gale and crying out, "I hear a voice that's speaking in the wind," and in a letter to Emily Sellwood he writes of "dim mystic sympathies with tree and hill reaching far back into childhood."[2] One feels the strong persistence of such sympathies throughout the Idylls. They are manifested less in individual details of natural description than in those larger movements of wind and earth and tide that reverberate throughout the poem and that the dying Arthur hears as "this great voice that shakes the world, / And wastes the narrow realm whereon we move" (PA, 139–140). Such landscapes are too vast for the human eye to contain, yet they are ever-present, in Santayana's words, "to that topographical sense by which we always live in the consciousness that there is a sea, that there are mountains, that the sky is above us, even when we do not see it, and that the tribes of men, with their different degrees of blamelessness, are scattered over the broad-backed earth. This cosmic landscape poetry alone can render."[3]

   The more closely one examines the Idylls, the more difficult it becomes to distinguish microcosm from macrocosm, character from landscape, foreground from background, symbol from thing symbolized. As David Palmer points out, a Tennysonian landscape is never merely a setting for the story but an image so highly charged with symbolic emotion "that in itself it seems to inspire the figures and events in the story . . . This mode of articulating feeling through the resonances of natural description was leading both poetry and painting towards the symbolist movement." [4] In the following passage Pelleas and the beggar are the only human actors, but the beggar, immobile and hunched "like an old dwarf-elm," has in fact lapsed back into nature, which acts as Pelleas' true antagonist, aroused to ominous life by Pelleas' brutality:

> Small pity upon his horse had he,
> Or on himself, or any, and when he met
> A cripple, one that held a hand for alms—
> Hunched as he was, and like an old dwarf-elm
> That turns its back on the salt blast, the boy
> Paused not, but overrode him, shouting, "False,
> And false with Gawain!" and so left him bruised
> And battered, and fled on, and hill and wood
> Went ever streaming by him till the gloom,
> That follows on the turning of the world
> Darkened the common path.
>
> (PE, 529–539)

In reeling back into the beast, Pelleas has violated his place in the natural hierarchy; this sense of unnatural reversal is conveyed by the movement of the landscape, which goes streaming past him. The moving landscape and fleeing Pelleas are in turn overshadowed by the diurnal rotation of the earth as it pivots toward darkness. "The gloom / That *follows* on the turning of the world" has the same ominous animation as the streaming landscape: the darkness seems to pursue Pelleas, cutting him off from the "common path" of humanity, from which he is a self-produced outcast.

We first see Pelleas as a knight-aspirant en route to

Camelot. He enters a grove which appears to be the archetype
of a pastoral paradise and the antithesis of the dark wood
through which he later flees. Half-dazed by the heat and
brilliance of the summer sun, he falls into a semisleep charged
with erotic fantasies of the maiden he longs to meet. Like
Adam, he awakens to find his dream of Eve come true:

> . . . he saw,
> Strange as to some old prophet might have seemed
> A vision hovering on a sea of fire,
> Damsels in divers colours like the cloud
> Of sunset and sunrise, and all of them
> On horses, and the horses richly trapt
> Breast-high in that bright line of bracken stood:
> And all the damsels talked confusedly,
> And one was pointing this way, and one that,
> Because the way was lost.
>
> (PE, 48–57)

In the midst of Pelleas' paradise, Tennyson intrudes a hint
of the infernal lake—the prophet's "sea of fire"—in which
Pelleas will later be consumed. The whole landscape seethes
with a surreal intensity of heat and light: the sun beats
like a sharp blow on Pelleas' helmet (22) and the ferns blaze
like "living fire of emeralds" (34). The prismatic splash of
color recalls the appearance, in the previous idyll, of the Grail
pulsing with color "as if alive" (HG, 118). Pelleas' erotic
vision in the glen is the carnal counterpart of the knights'
vision of the Holy Grail, and Arthur's prophecy that the
Grail knights will "follow wandering fires / Lost in the
quagmire" (HG, 319–320) finds its literal fulfillment in
Pelleas' death in the marshes. Like the Grail knights, the
"errant" damsels whom Pelleas sees on awakening have lost
their way, but their goal, as Ettarre makes clear in a punning
parody of the Grail quest, is a sexual tilt with Arthur's
warriors:

> Youth, we are damsels-errant, and we ride,

Armed as ye see, to tilt against the knights
There at Caerleon, but have lost our way.

(61–63)

Pelleas mistakes the degenerate Ettarre for the ideal damsel
of his dreams, but those dreams mask a crudely undirected
sexuality that makes Ettarre instantly and obsessively
attractive to him. His naive romanticism has its rank
underside, just as the idyllic landscape reveals on closer
inspection a diseased luxuriance. The very profuseness of
Ettarre's garden, with its tiers of roses overgrown with
brambles, suggests the disorderliness of excess. And Ettarre's
too-easy accessibility is more than hinted at by the "wide
open" gates of her castle (405) and the "yawning" entrance
leading to her private grounds (412).[5] After discovering
Ettarre asleep with Gawain, Pelleas rides in fury from her
castle, whose towers silhouetted against the moon loom up as
a kind of distorted enlargement of her body; Ettarre and the
landscape merge in Pelleas' disordered mind into a composite
image of sexual menace:

And forth he past, and mounting on his horse
Stared at her towers that, larger than themselves
In their own darkness, thronged into the moon.
Then crushed the saddle with his thighs, and clenched
His hands, and maddened with himself . . .*

(447–451)

Pelleas moves from a state of idealistic illusion to savage
disillusion. The landscape undergoes a parallel reversal from

---

* With odd obtuseness Browning objected to these lines as irrelevant
decoration: "We look at the art of poetry so differently! Here is an
Idyll about a knight being untrue to his friend and yielding to the
temptation of his friend's mistress after having engaged to assist
him in his suit. I should judge the conflict of the knight's soul the
proper subject to describe. Tennyson thinks he should describe the
castle, and the effect of the moon on its towers, and anything
but the soul." (Letter to Isa Blagden, cited in J. Philip Eggers, *King
Arthur's Laureate: A Study of Tennyson's "Idylls of the King"* [New
York, New York University Press, 1971], p. 69.) Mistaking Gawain

pastoral romance to the topography of nightmare, with
frightening castles, dwarfish cripples, and predatory beasts.
Pelleas loses his identity in the infernal wood and
reconstitutes himself as Arthur's enemy, the nameless Red
Knight of the North. In this guise he reappears in "The Last
Tournament," where he boasts that he has achieved the
integrity of absolute dissoluteness, unlike the hypocrite
adulterers and harlots of Arthur's court. Pelleas and the
landscape in which he now establishes his counter-kingdom
are in perfect harmony. To reach his sworn enemy, Arthur
leads his young knights through a wilderness of rank
marshes; there the drunken Pelleas lunges savagely at Arthur,
stumbles into the mire, and the knights

> leapt down upon the fallen;
> There trampled out his face from being known,
> And sank his head in mire, and slimed themselves.
> (LT, 468–470)

With grotesque appropriateness the anonymous Red Knight
is trampled into featurelessness. The attackers and the thing
attacked have alike reverted to beasts sunk in the primordial
slime. Anticipating the confused oaths and slaughter of
the Last Battle, the knights massacre Pelleas' women and set
fire to his hall, until the surrounding meres glow with
blood-red flames, like

> the water Moab saw[6]
> Come round by the East, and out beyond them flushed
> The long low dune, and lazy-plunging sea.
> (LT, 481–483)

---

for the protagonist of the idyll, Browning also failed to see that the
conflict in Pelleas' soul is perfectly rendered by the hallucinatory
description of the castle. The lapse is the more remarkable in that
both Browning and Tennyson excelled in revealing character without
relying on the conventions of stage-drama; landscape serves to
dramatize and define character in the *Idylls* precisely as the Renaissance
setting illuminates the character of Browning's Duke of Ferrara or
Fra Lippo Lippi.

The fiery setting and the opening out of the landscape into
low dunes foreshadow the land "upheaven from the abyss /
By fire," where Arthur's host engages Modred's along an
amorphous coast of ever-shifting sands (PA, 82–87). The end
of Pelleas' career is radically different from its start, but
the end is contained in the beginning: "Suddenly wakened
with a sound of talk" (46),

>   . . . he saw,
> Strange as to some old prophet might have seemed
> A vision hovering on a sea of fire.
>
>   (PE, 48–50)

The three characters in the *Idylls* who suffer madness—
Pelleas, Balin, and Lancelot—all flee the court and withdraw
into wild woods or wastelands. Only Lancelot emerges from
the ordeal alive. His survival results from an act of will
in consonance with a gift of grace. He strays from the
common path but finds the strength to cut his way out of the
wilderness. Balin and Pelleas are victims of a prior flaw
which turns their wills against themselves and renders them
powerless to resist the hostile landscape that finally entombs
them, and that is at once their enemy and themselves.

Of those who enter the wilderness, only Gareth returns
wholly unscathed, as befits the one character in the *Idylls*
whose undivided will reduces all dangers to harmless
phantoms. Geraint's strangely enervated will—his manhood
is "molten down in mere uxoriousness" (MG, 60)—renders
him incapable of resisting the perils of the hostile forest
in which, appropriately, he bleeds "underneath his armour
secretly" (GE, 502). The inner debility of Geraint contrasts
strikingly with his powerful body, with its "massive square"
of heroic breast and knotted muscles which protrude even
as he sleeps (MG, 75–78). A parallel disparity is reflected
in the landscape, which combines a surface beauty with an
underlying tension and uncertainty, like the strained smile of

Geraint himself, which Tennyson compares to "a stormy sunlight" (GE, 480).

The peculiarly mixed quality of the landscape in turn reflects the intermediate position of the Geraint idylls, poised between the happy marriage of Gareth and Lynette and the fratricide of Balin and Balan. Although set in the heat of summer, much of the action occurs in lightless thickets or inside the decaying castle of Yniol and the gloomy hall of Doorm, a kind of Cro-Magnon Camelot. Only once is the pastoral luxuriance of the season fully felt, when Geraint and Enid emerge from the "green gloom" of the woods,

> And issuing under open heavens beheld
> A little town with towers, upon a rock,
> And close beneath, a meadow gemlike chased
> In the brown wild, and mowers mowing in it . . .
>   (GE, 196–199)

For the most part they traverse trackless wastes, and once they come upon a scene of utter desolation prophetic of the "fragments of forgotten peoples" at the site of the Last Battle. Earl Doorm lies dead, and his people are scattered over a field,

> Where, huddled here and there on mound and knoll,
> Were men and women staring and aghast,
> While some yet fled . . .
>   (GE, 802–804)

The Geraint idylls, as J. Philip Eggers observes, leave the reader subtly troubled, as if the landscape were pulling like a tide against the optimistic line of the story: nature everywhere appears "elusive and uncertain," an effect achieved through the omnipresent imagery of "slipping, falling, losing, darting, flashing, and rippling."[7] Enid dreams of "slipping down horrible precipices," Earl Limours' faithless cohorts desert him like fish darting from a sudden shadow cast in a stream, and one of Geraint's adversaries

falls like a great piece of promontory sliding into the sea
(GE, 379, 467–475, 162–164). As if to underscore the moral
symbolism of these unstable landscapes, Edyrn exclaims
on being overthrown by Geraint, "My pride is broken: men
have seen my fall" (MG, 578), a fall later reenacted by the
wounded Geraint as he tumbles wordlessly from his
horse (GE, 508).[8]

Like the landscapes in which he figures, Geraint's nature
is highly ambiguous. Although handsome, powerful, and
fiercely possessive of his wife, he is not only uxorious but also
curiously uncertain of his sexuality. "Yourself shall see my
vigour is not lost," he cries out to Enid, and his companions-
in-arms speak derisively of how his former force has given
way to "mere effeminacy" (GE, 83; MG, 106–107). For
all his prowess in arms, he is something of a dandy and
arrives late for the jousts adorned in a flowing scarf of purple
and gold (MG, 165–170). Violent yet indolent, fastidious
yet gluttonous, he eats "with all the passion of a twelve
hours' fast" and ravens down the meal that the mower
provides out of his own scant store (MG, 306; GE, 212–215).
These details of characterization appear superfluous in a
story whose characters, after all, have little psychological
depth. Yet they are central to Tennyson's design, for once
Geraint enters the wilderness it is his own divided self that he
encounters in the contrasting personas of the effeminate
Limours and the brutal, gluttonous Doorm. Like Geraint, the
"femininely fair" and "all-amorous," Limours (compare
l'amour) dotes upon Enid, just as the gross Earl Doorm, again
like Geraint, tyrannizes over her (GE, 275, 360). Both
Limours and Doorm are extensions of Geraint's erotic
obsession with Enid; the dangers of that obsession, now
grown to pathological proportions in the rank wilderness, are
symbolized by Geraint's near-fatal struggle with them both.

Yet even after perceiving the design of the Geraint idylls,
one feels that Tennyson's intention has been imperfectly
realized. That design is too complex for the naive human

agents who figure in it. One is reminded of Harold Nicolson's impatient judgment, uttered with the fine, reckless license of old age, "Geraint is a cad and Enid is a noodle."[9] Among the earliest composed of the idylls, "The Marriage of Geraint" and "Geraint and Enid" represent an intermediate stage in Tennyson's development, before he had evolved a narrative form which could bear the weight of the symbolic landscapes and doublings of identity that he perfected in "Pelleas and Ettarre" and "Balin and Balan."[10] Then, too, the very structure of the *Idylls*, with each section cumulatively enriching those that precede it, inevitably places the earlier sections at a disadvantage. "Gareth and Lynette" overcomes this disadvantage by being surreptitiously retold as "Pelleas and Ettarre," whereas the Geraint idylls, despite their evident thematic connections with what follows, remain largely self-contained.

This lack of resonance is most apparent in passages of merely ornamental description, such as the elaborate double simile comparing Enid's voice to that of a nightingale and Geraint to

> a man abroad at morn
> When first the liquid note beloved of men
> Comes flying over many a windy wave
> To Britain, and in April suddenly
> Breaks from a coppice gemmed with green and red,
> And he suspends his converse with a friend,
> Or it may be the labour of his hands,
> To think or say, "There is the nightingale."
> (MG, 335–342)

The landscape does not draw us more deeply into the world of the *Idylls* but, in its meticulous picturesqueness, imitates a Victorian narrative painting. The sentimentality, the hearthside décor and sententiousness of much of the writing —"Our hoard is little, but our hearts are great" (MG, 374)— suggest that Tennyson was still under the cloying shadow of the domestic idylls.

Yet there are passages of unquestionable power in the
Geraint idylls, and these invariably occur when the landscape
serves not as a decorative embellishment but as a naturalized
symbol of the moral condition of the realm. Doorm's
scattered retinue, huddled here and there on mound and
knoll, provides an example. A more striking instance occurs
as Geraint comes upon Yniol's half-ruined castle. The litter
of disjointed stones prefigures the wreckage of Camelot
after the Grail quest, when the returning knights stumble
over cracked basilisks and hornless unicorns:

> Then rode Geraint into the castle court,
> His charger trampling many a prickly star
> Of sprouted thistle on the broken stones.
>   . . . monstrous ivy-stems
> Claspt the gray walls with hairy-fibred arms,
> And sucked the joining of the stones, and looked
> A knot, beneath, of snakes, aloft, a grove.
>   (MG, 312–314, 322–325)

"Balin and Balan," the next in sequence but last-composed
of the idylls, most clearly exemplifies the interpenetration
of character and setting. The landscape is a spatialization of
Balin's consciousness, Balin the animate point at which the
landscape comes into focus. The dualities within Balin are
reflected in the dualities without; conversely, Balin symbolizes
the warring elements that are wrecking the realm: the
contest between the King and chaos, garden and wilderness,
music and discord, reason and bestiality. The idyll opens with
the two brothers posed like twin statues beside the
"carolling" fountain. The perfect symmetry of the tableau,
the balanced phrasing, the virtual identity of the names,
all hint from the start that the two brothers are in fact
dissevered halves of the same self:

> So coming to the fountain-side [Arthur] beheld
> Balin and Balan sitting statuelike,

Brethren, to right and left the spring, that down,
From underneath a plume of lady-fern,
Sang, and the sand danced at the bottom of it.
And on the right of Balin Balin's horse
Was fast beside an alder, on the left
Of Balan Balan's near a poplar tree.

(21–28)

Their first words are spoken in chorus (30–34) and their
last words, as they embrace in death—"Good night, true
brother"—are identical (614–616). With a single exception
(the word *I*), Balan never addresses a character other than
his twin.[11] Balin serves as spokesman for them both at
court; his subordinate self, Balan, remains mute except in
debate with himself or with Balin. An exceptionally high
proportion of the dialogue of both brothers is in fact interior
monologue—the self, appropriately, addressing itself.

Exiled from the court for striking one of Arthur's knights,
Balin has been restrained by Balan from further violence
during his "kingless years" (61). Arthur welcomes Balin back
to the Round Table in words that serve to medicine his mind
and echo the music first heard at the founding of Camelot:

Rise, my true knight. As children learn, be thou
Wiser for falling! walk with me, and move
To music with thine Order and the King.*

(72–74)

The opening of the idyll centers on images of order and
harmony: the caroling waters, Arthur's restorative words,
the choral welcome the knights sing as Balin the Savage, "an
unmelodious name" (50), rejoins them. The court figures

* From the Trinity College Library MS. of "Balin and Balan" it is
clear that the important last line of this quotation occurred to Tennyson
after he had completed the first draft of the poem. The interpolation
serves to stress the motif of music versus discord that is especially
prominent in "Balin and Balan" and that runs throughout the *Idylls*.
Again, one is struck by how much of the thematic unity of the poem
was achieved through revision.

as a kind of well-ordered garden in which Balin seeks to
retune his jangled senses. He patterns himself on Lancelot's
courtesy, replaces the rough heraldic beast on his shield with
the Queen's royal crest, and with Balan ever-present in the
background, feels "his being move / In music with his
Order, and the King" (207–208).

Beyond the court lies a demon-haunted wood, and when
Balan undertakes to slay the human fiend who inhabits it, he
warns Balin:

> Let not thy moods prevail, when I am gone
> Who used to lay them! hold them outer fiends,
> Who leap at thee to tear thee; shake them aside,
> Dreams ruling when wit sleeps!
>
> (137–140)

With the parting of the two brothers, Balin's "heats and
violences" (186) threaten to return, for his rational self has
abandoned him and the dreams that rule when reason sleeps
break into his waking life. Like Merlin who "walked with
dreams and darkness" before his fall (MV, 188), Balin is
peculiarly ripe for the shock that confronts him when he sees
Lancelot and Guinevere together in the Queen's garden.
Later, in the parallel scene of lovers discovered in a rose
garden, Pelleas undergoes the same shock. As if recoiling
from their own suppressed desires, Balin and Pelleas react not
with accusation but with guilt and violent self-contempt.
"I . . . am not worthy to be knight; / A churl, a clown!"
(279–281) Balin exclaims. And Pelleas, as if he had "[felt] a
snake" (PE, 428), creeps in shame from the sleeping Gawain
and Ettarre. Gardens in the *Idylls* have lost their primal
innocence, and the flights of Balin and Pelleas into the
wilderness represent their attempts to find a world in more
apparent accord than Camelot with their newfound
experience of evil. "Queen? subject?" Balin asks; "but I see
not what I see. / Damsel and lover? hear not what I hear. /
. . . and in him gloom on gloom / Deepened" (276–282).

As Pelleas achieves a kind of ironic integrity through dissolution in the mire, so Balin finds his essential self in the demonic woods. He enters the forest at precisely the point where Balan has preceded him, but now, disjoined from the twin who suppressed the fiends that arose within him, he rides in fury through a hellish landscape emblematic of his darkened mind. Grabbing an axe from an ancient woodman who stands, Charon-like, at the entrance to this underworld, Balin chops through a bough in a single blow: "Lord," exclaims the woodman, "thou couldst lay the Devil of these woods / If arm of flesh could lay him!" (293–294). But Balin is powerless to slay him, for this demon is beyond the reach of flesh and lodges in Balin himself, as he perceives: "To lay that devil would lay the Devil in me" (296). Blind to everything except the chained rage "which ever yelpt within" (314), he rides past a yawning cavern where tusklike rocks rise from the ground and then bursts his lance against a forest bough, rendering himself impotent, like Pelleas, who leaves his sword across the naked throats of Gawain and Ettarre.

In the middle of his journey Balin comes upon the bat-infested castle of King Pellam and his mysterious "heir," Garlon, who has been pursuing Balin like a shadow through the forest. The setting is fraught with menace as the unarmed Balin enters the dim banquet hall and the

> . . . leaves
> Laid their green faces flat against the panes,
> Sprays grated, and the cankered boughs without
> Whined in the wood.
>   (338–341)

Balin's hostile and mocking hosts are in essence projections of his suppressed self, as Limours and Doorm in a similar setting are projections of Geraint. Pellam, formerly "a Christless foe" of Arthur's, has undergone a dubious conversion and affects an asceticism so repressive that he has

banished all women, including his wife, from his gates
(94–104). The heir of Pellam's repressed sexuality is the
slanderous and lascivious Garlon, a clandestine lover of
Vivien's who serves as her double in defaming the Queen to
Balin. When Balin later believes that slander, he falls prey
to the Garlon within himself.

Stage by stage, as Balin recedes into the "savage woods"
(479), he reverts further into bestiality until, discarding the
shield with Guinevere's crest, he becomes the living emblem
of the rough beast, "toothed with grinning savagery"
(193), originally emblazoned on his shield. Reality and
symbol have exchanged identities, just as character and
landscape have merged. Hanging his shield high on a branch,
Balin

> turned aside into the woods,
> And there in gloom cast himself all along,
> Moaning, "My violences, my violences!"
>
> (427–429)

The ambiguous "in gloom" applies with equal weight to the
skyless forest and to Balin's darkened consciousness.

Totally vulnerable, Balin encounters Vivien the instant he
abandons his shield. It is as if the Queen's crest has until
now served as a talisman, warding off Vivien's entrance into
the idyll until Guinevere has made her exit. With that exit
Vivien silences "the wholesome music of the wood" (430)
by singing her own potent, pagan hymn to the generative
fire of nature:

> The fire of Heaven is on the dusty ways.
> The wayside blossoms open to the blaze.
> The whole wood-world is one full peal of praise.
> The fire of Heaven is not the flame of Hell.
>
> The fire of Heaven is lord of all things good,
> And starve not thou this fire within thy blood,

But follow Vivien through the fiery flood!
The fire of Heaven is not the flame of Hell!

(442–449)

Vivien's "old sun-worship" will soon drown out the music of
Arthur's Order; we see its first effects in the person of Balin,
whom she destroys by slander, as she later destroys Merlin
through seduction. Until encountering Vivien, Balin had
turned in upon himself the violence reawakened by his
discovery of Lancelot and Guinevere in the garden. Their
adultery is still unproven, very likely as yet unconsummated,
but Vivien lies "with ease" (517) and, although Balin has
previously fought back the evidence of his own senses, he
instantly believes her slander. Wholly possessed, he tramples
the royal crest to pieces and utters a "weird yell, /
Unearthlier than all shriek of bird or beast" (535–536).
Mistaking the bestial cry for the wood-demon he has sworn
to slay, Balan attacks Balin and each brother mortally
wounds the other.

On the simple narrative level, coincidence and confusion
of identity provide a dénouement rich in the pathos of
romance. But on a deeper level Balan is not at all mistaken:
Balin *is* in fact the wood-demon, the "outer fiend" whom
Balan finally lays to rest. We first see the two brothers as
mirror images of each other moving in harmony to the music
of Arthur's Order. When Balin's violence returns, they
split apart and as Balin recedes further into the wilderness,
the two selves become progressively alienated. Disjoined by
violence, they are rejoined in violence. In the Freudian
terms the tale inevitably suggests, repression has failed, and
the rational self can control the savage self only by destroying
it. The unwitting fratricide is in reality a symbolic suicide.
The point is subtly underscored by the actual cause of the
brothers' death. Balin's spear pierces Balan's flesh, but Balin
is slain by the bestiality within himself, as symbolized by
his wearied horse, which fell upon him and "crushed the
man / Inward" (553–554). "My madness all thy life has

been thy doom," the dying Balin tells his twin, who answers in echo, "We two were born together, and we die / Together by one doom" (608, 617–618).

Throughout the idyll the reader senses an ironic incongruity between Balin's physical and psychological maturity. His "too fierce manhood" (71) masks a childlike aggressiveness which finds its counterpart in his need for absolute submissiveness, as in his hero-worship of Lancelot. The whole of "Balin and Balan" may be read as a story of failed initiation in which one aspect of the hero, Balan, rises to adulthood and the other half, Balin, regresses to infancy. After overthrowing Balin at the fountain, Arthur says, "As children learn, be thou / Wiser for falling!" (72–73), and it is as a fallen child that Balin makes his halting efforts to rejoin Arthur's Order. At their moment of death both brothers make the journey back through time, Balin "crawling" slowly to Balan, Balan "with a childlike wail" kissing Balin (581, 585). Seated side by side at the start of the idyll, they are even more intimately joined at its end, "either locked in either's arm."*

In "Balin and Balan" and "Pelleas and Ettarre" the demonic landscape symbolizes an individual aberration of mind. In "The Holy Grail" and "The Last Tournament" the landscape reflects a general condition of the realm. The violent tempest in "The Holy Grail" strikes at all the characters, including

---

* In bk. II of *Le Morte d'Arthur* Balin le Savage is "a poor knight with King Arthur" who, despite repeated acts of courage and kindness, succeeds only in wreaking evil on those he tries to befriend. After a rambling series of misadventures, he at last encounters his younger brother Balan, whom he unwittingly attacks, each brother slaying the other. Tennyson follows the broad outline of Malory's story but cuts through a forest of irrelevancies. His brooding imagination seizes the archetypal heart of the matter which underlies Malory's tale but which Malory evidently had not perceived: Balin le Savage, ever attempting good but doing evil, becomes in Tennyson's hands a victim not of external ill-fortune but of a fatally divided self, at war with the uncontrollable violence within, and, finally, the self-slain victim of that violence. Hence Balin and Balan, who are merely

Arthur, and devastates Camelot itself. Both timescape and landscape are apocalyptic: ancient trees spring into fire, the heavens blaze, and in a matter of moments the city suffers the damage of centuries. The less violent storm in "The Last Tournament" is not supernatural in origin but marks a natural phase in the accelerating decline of the realm. The tournament takes place to the accompaniment of autumn thunder, drenching rains, and a winnowing wind that blows through all of the remaining idylls and does not cease until Arthur's death. The trumpet summoning the combatants rings with a muffled blast suggestive of distant judgment:

> The sudden trumpet sounded as in a dream
> To ears but half-awaked, then one low roll
> O' Autumn thunder, and the jousts began:
> And ever the wind blew, and yellowing leaf
> And gloom and gleam, and shower and shorn plume
> Went down it.
>
> (151–156)

Lancelot, who presides over the tournament in Arthur's absence, sees all the rules of courtesy broken and with bitter grace awards the prize to Tristram. The ruby carcanet, found around the neck of an abandoned child, gives to the contest the title "The Tournament of Dead Innocence." Guinevere had adopted the child but she soon died, for

---

brothers in Malory and whose deaths are not simultaneous, become *twins* in Tennyson, born and slain at the same moment.

Despite Tennyson's ingenuity and profundity in re-creating the story of Balin and Balan, the idyll has fared very badly in the hands of the critics. Cf. this gathering of epithets by J. M. Gray, who observes that "critics who write of Balin's 'rather confused and unintelligible adventures,' of the poet's 'perversity of judgment,' of his substituting 'another form of incoherence,' and of the 'abominable wreckage' that he has made of Malory's story have all too often confused the two." (Gray, *Tennyson's Doppelgänger: "Balin and Balan,"* Tennyson Society Monographs, no. 3 [Lincoln, Eng., The Tennyson Society, 1971], p. 8.) Gray is currently writing what promises to be the first comprehensive modern study of the *Idylls* in relation to its sources.

innocence can no longer survive at Camelot. The realm has fallen into the sere and yellow leaf, and the sterility of the season finds its analogue in the sterility of all the major characters. Although the old order passes and Tristram, like Vivien, sings of new life and new love, in the human world there is no regeneration. Early in the poem Geraint and Enid produce "Enids and Geraints / Of times to be" (GE, 964–965), but their time never comes; they are stillborn fictions whose sole function is to terminate the idyll in which they appear. The only children of Guinevere, as Arthur says in his bitterest lines, are "sword and fire, / Red ruin, and the breaking up of laws" (G, 422–423). Like Arthur and Guinevere, Tristram and Isolt are childless, and Lancelot dies wifeless and heirless, as do the sensual Gawain and the ascetic Galahad. Balin and Pelleas, late recruits to the Round Table, are rendered impotent and then slain, and Vivien, who also comes late to court, was born on a battlefield alongside the corpse of her father and expends all of her sexual energies in destroying the kingdom.

Tristram enters this sterile world in armor of forest green, with spear, harp, and bugle emblazoned on his shield. Hunter and musician, he seems incongruously vital amidst the languid decadence of the court. He is the bearer of the "new philosophy" of naturalism, disdains the older niceties of combat, and as he gains his easy victory one of the ladies of the court says, "All courtesy is dead," and another, "The glory of our Round Table is no more" (LT, 211–212). The decline of the court and of the season are in such close accord that each seems the natural consequence of the other. But as there are two orders of time in the *Idylls*, so there are two orders of landscape, and overriding the autumnal setting of "The Last Tournament" is a more sinister landscape filled with portents of the Last Battle. The muffled trumpet-blast echoes forward to the trumpet that summons Arthur to his doom (G, 526), and the maimed churl whom Pelleas sends to Camelot at the start of the tournament personifies the fragments of forgotten peoples who will inherit Arthur's kingdom after it has reeled back into the beast. The challenge the churl bears from the Red Knight—

> say [Arthur's] hour is come,
> The heathen are upon him, his long lance
> Broken, and his Excalibur a straw—
>
> (86–88)

carries one step closer to fulfillment Vivien's prophecy that her old sun-worship will "beat the cross to earth, and break the King / And all his Table" (BB, 452–453). The prophecy seems momentarily reversed when Arthur stems the "ever-climbing wave" of heathen who "make their last head like Satan in the North" (LT, 92, 98). But the King's ambiguous victory is soiled by his own knights who, in their massacre of the Red Knight and all his women, reenact a second and far more savage Tournament of Dead Innocence.

The sense of doom overhanging "The Last Tournament" carries over directly from the close of "Pelleas and Ettarre." Pelleas attacks Lancelot and rides through the court like a maddened beast:

> The Queen
> Looked hard upon her lover, he on her;
> And each foresaw the dolorous day to be:
> And all talk died, as in a grove all song
> Beneath the shadow of some bird of prey;
> Then a long silence came upon the hall,
> And Modred thought, "The time is hard at hand."
>
> (PE, 591–597)

Modred, like Vivien, is a quoter of Scripture, and his "thought" alludes to Jesus' warning to the disciples, "My time is at hand."[12] The Red Knight's challenge in "The Last Tournament"—"say his hour is come"—in turn echoes both Modred's line and Jesus' "The hour is come."[13] The predatory bird that shadows the close of "Pelleas and

Ettarre" reappears at the start of "The Last Tournament."
As Arthur leaves Camelot he confesses to Lancelot his fears
that the realm, upreared by noble vows, will "reel back into
the beast, and be no more";[14] on the eve of the tournament,
the King's fears haunt Lancelot's sleep, and circling round
his "sick head all night, like birds of prey, / The words of
Arthur flying shrieked" (138–139).

Neither oppressed, like Lancelot, by his failure to keep the
vows, nor obsessed, like Pelleas, by the compulsion to
break them, Tristram appears wholly untroubled by the
darker portents that circle over Camelot. He rides carefree
through the "slowly mellowing" lanes toward Tintagil, and
with his crest of holly spray "Sir Tristram of the Woods"
(177) seems a part of the forest itself. With animal keenness
his eye is alert to "all that walked, or crept, or perched"
(367). Only once, when Tristram dreams that the ruby
necklace has turned into frozen blood (412), does Tennyson
hint that the hunter is in fact the hunted, and only once does
Tristram's alertness fail, and then fatally, when Mark
cleaves him from behind.

At Tintagil Isolt receives Tristram in her tower like a
disillusioned Elaine greeting a degraded Lancelot: "thou,
through ever harrying thy wild beasts / . . . art grown wild
beast thyself" (630, 632). As Isolt sits gazing out over the
Western seas, the landscape detaches itself from the autumn
woods, from Arthur's kingdom, from time and place, and
opens out upon an unending horizon symbolic of her own
longing for death:

> hour by hour,
> Here in the never-ended afternoon,
> O sweeter than all memories of thee,
> Deeper than any yearnings after thee
> Seemed those far-rolling, westward-smiling seas.
> (579–583)

Drugged by isolation and sustained in life only by her hatred

of Mark, Isolt is imprisoned in a landscape virtually
indistinguishable from that of "The Lotos-Eaters," whose
weary cadences she echoes:

> In the afternoon they came unto a land
> In which it seemèd always afternoon.
> All round the coast the languid air did swoon,
> Breathing like one that hath a weary dream.
>
> · · ·
>
> Give us long rest or death, dark death, or dreamful ease.
>   ("The Lotos-Eaters," 3–6, 98)

Although the actions crowded into "The Last Tournament"
occupy only a few days, the setting and imagery range widely
through all the reaches of the kingdom. The idyll opens
with the Fool dancing like a withered leaf before the hall of
Camelot, shifts in setting to the woods of Lyonnesse where
Tristram dreams of his two Isolts, to the northern wastes
where Arthur slays the Red Knight, to the westernmost seas
surrounding Tintagil, and, with dramatic suddenness, back
again to Camelot. As Mark murders Tristram, the twilit vistas
of Tintagil yield to the claustrophobic darkness of Arthur's
return—"All in a death-dumb autumn-dripping gloom"
(750)—to the empty chamber of the Queen. The line is more
than an exercise in the onomatopoeia of decay. Tristram dies
"death-dumb" like a slaughtered animal, and the Red Knight
topples wordless and sodden into the mire. The "dumbness"
of the autumn also symbolizes the silencing of Arthur's music,
first heard at the founding of Camelot, muted by Vivien's
pagan hymn, further fractured into discord by Tristram's
song, and now heard only in the muffled music of the Fool,
who greets the returning King with inarticulate sobs. The Fool
has been made a mock-knight and in his folly tries to attune
himself to Arthur's Order at a time when all the true knights
have proven false. And so when Tristram sings of "new
life, new love" (279), the Fool chides him for making false
music with Queen Isolt and persists in dancing "to the broken

music of [his] brains" (258), until at the idyll's end he too
has become "death-dumb." The "autumn-dripping gloom"
harks back to the thick rains of the opening and to the
"gloom on gloom" that deepens in Balin and Pelleas and now
overcomes Arthur, who is himself caught up in the darkening
confusion of the realm.

As Arthur's purposes are progressively defeated, the
landscape of the closing idylls becomes more and more obscure.
The mists that enshroud the Last Battle contrast with the
preternatural clarity of the first battle in the "Coming of
Arthur," when the King establishes his sovereignty over his
foes. The bright pavilions of the opposing forces stand
sharply etched on the field, and the world

> Was all so clear about him, that he saw
> The smallest rock far on the faintest hill,
> And even in high day the morning star.
>
> (97–99)

The combat takes on the stylized clarity of a medieval
illumination—"so like a painted battle the war stood" (121)—
and the setting mirrors the self-assurance of the King. "Thou
dost not doubt me King," Arthur calls in victory to Lancelot,
who cries back,

> "the fire of God
> Descends upon thee in the battle-field:
> I know thee for my King!"
>
> (125, 127–129)

In the parallel scene in the Last Battle, confusion supplants
clarity as the sea washes over the dead, eating away at the
narrow strand on which only Arthur and Bedivere remain
alive. The "space" which the King cleared has dwindled to
this shrinking strip of coast. Amidst the muffled tumult, the
half-seen dead faces and hollow helmets awash on the coast,

in this world of nightmare illusion and deathly reality, Arthur confronts the final nightmare of self-doubt:

> "Hearest thou this great voice that shakes the world,
> And wastes the narrow realm whereon we move,
> And beats upon the faces of the dead,
> My dead, as though they had not died for me?—
> O Bedivere, for on my heart hath fallen
> Confusion, till I know not what I am,
> Nor whence I am, nor whether I be King.
> Behold, I seem but King among the dead."
>
> (139–146)

The King is in the "place of tombs," his watery Golgotha.[15] Mortally wounded and moving ghostlike through the mists, he is never more real than when so ghostly. Arthur is at once the central and most elusive figure in the *Idylls*, a presence whose reality has always been equivocal. He is the point of focus at which the idealisms of all the other characters converge, and as their structure of conviction breaks down, Arthur and his kingdom vanish along with it. In this sense, the King is brought into being by the vows sworn and the deeds done in his name. As Arthur creates an Order, so his knights reciprocally create Arthur in their own best image: "They prove to him his work," Guinevere says in a rare moment of insight into the King (LE, 157). But the essence of the King's work is that it can never be proven, and it remains one of the great open questions of the *Idylls* whether the King and his city are real, or the aboriginal wastes that finally envelop them.

Throughout the *Idylls* dreams are the enigmatic mediators of Arthur's reality. Landscapes of the mind unbound by the literalisms of time and place, they at once prophesy and reenact the King's self-doubts in "The Passing of Arthur." The dream of Leodogran in "The Coming of Arthur" figures as a kind of "little apocalypse" foreshadowing Arthur's uncertainties as he surveys the dead strewn about the

battlefield. Leodogran dreams of "a phantom king" hidden
in a haze of rolling flames; the shouts of men slaughtering
each other and crying out against his rule drown out the
King's voice. Suddenly the dream changes, the haze lifts,

> and the solid earth became
> As nothing, but the King stood out in heaven,
> Crowned.*
>
> (CA, 441–443)

The two halves of the dream have no logical connection,
except as mutually contradictory opposites, and either half
may be taken as a valid prophecy of Arthur's fate. That
Leodogran chooses to support the King is as arbitrary as
Gareth's affirming Arthur's reality even as Camelot
disappears in mist before his eyes and Merlin warns that the
King, like his city, may be only "a shadow" (GL, 262).
Throughout the poem substance and shadow change places,
and it is Arthur's peculiarity as a character that the shadow
he casts is more real than his substance. Hence it is that
in "Guinevere" he is unconvincing in his role as injured
husband, but the moment he is back in his true setting—the
death-white mists of the Last Battle—he takes on an
overwhelming reality. As part of the same paradox, he is
absent when the Grail is seen, present in its absence, for the
two equivocally "real presences" might be mutually
annihilatory. Or perhaps Arthur *is* the Grail and opposes
the quest because he is already among them but they know
him not. As soon as the Grail passes, Arthur returns to

---

* Tennyson emphasizes the suddenness and mystery of the change
with the words "Till with a wink his dream was changed" (440).
The line alludes to I Corinthians 15, in which Paul writes, "Behold,
I shew you a mystery; We shall not all sleep, but we shall all be changed,
In a moment, in the twinkling of an eye, at the last trump: for the
trumpet shall sound, and the dead shall be raised incorruptible"
(51–52). The total reversal in Leodogran's dream from the imperiled,
earthbound King to the heavenly King crowned in glory is as abrupt
as the transition in Corinthians from death to immortality.

speak, in words which recall Leodogran's dream, of his own visions, when

> this earth he walks on seems not earth,
> This light that strikes his eyeball is not light,
> This air that smites his forehead is not air
> But vision—yea, his very hand and foot—
> In moments when he feels he cannot die,
> And knows himself no vision to himself,
> Nor the high God a vision, nor that One
> Who rose again . . .
>
> (HG, 908–915)

The landscape of "The Holy Grail" carries into the actual narrative of the *Idylls* the topography of dreams and combines elements of nightmare—snakes, human bones, stinking swamps—with visions of the celestial city. The quest is at once a disaster and a revelation: the sacred mount of Camelot falls into ruins, yet in Percivale's vision of the Grail the heavenly city on which Camelot is patterned is seen in perfect clarity for the one and only time:

> . . . "I saw the least of little stars
> Down on the waste, and straight beyond the star
> I saw the spiritual city and all her spires
> And gateways in a glory like one pearl." [16]
>
> (524–527)

Camelot partakes of the dual reality of the holy city of Revelation, of which it is a replica, and the Infernal City, the Great Whore of Babylon, which it has become. Pelleas has modeled his anti-Camelot of the North on this Infernal City, and his dream of Camelot's fiery destruction portends the end of his own city as well as Arthur's, both of which, like the Great Babylon, are "utterly burned with fire." [17] The two cities merge in Pelleas' mind after he discovers Gawain's treachery and, exhausted by his wild ride through the forest, he

> gulfed his griefs in inmost sleep; so lay,
> Till shaken by a dream, that Gawain fired
> The hall of Merlin, and the morning star
> Reeled in the smoke, brake into flame, and fell.
>
> (PE, 506–509)

Guinevere's dream in the convent at Almesbury comes so close in time to the event it foretells that it serves less as prophecy than as prologue to the closing idylls. The flaming sunset symbolizes the end of the realm, and the avenging shadow that lengthens at her feet is her own guilt, come to haunt her nights of repentance and envelop the whole kingdom:

> . . . she dreamed
> An awful dream; for then she seemed to stand
> On some vast plain before a setting sun,
> And from the sun there swiftly made at her
> A ghastly something, and its shadow flew
> Before it, till it touched her, and she turned—
> When lo! her own, that broadening from her feet,
> And blackening, swallowed all the land, and in it
> Far cities burnt, and with a cry she woke.[18]
>
> (G, 74–82)

Earlier in the *Idylls* Gareth had referred to Arthur as the "great Sun of Glory" (GL, 22), and in "Lancelot and Elaine" Guinevere, condemning the King for the fault of his faultlessness, had asked, "But who can gaze upon the Sun in heaven?" (123). Whoever loves her must, like Lancelot, have "a touch of earth," for "the low sun makes the colour; I am yours, / Not Arthur's" (133–135). Now that the King and Lancelot are warring against each other and Guinevere finally recognizes that she is Arthur's, the "low sun" of her passion, like the red of her rose garden, comes back to her in horror. On the eve of his transfiguration Arthur assumes in her eyes a humanity far greater than he has ever had. If Guinevere lacks the insight to interpret her dream, the King does so for her moments later, when he appears in the convent as the personified Sun of Glory and damns her legacy of red ruin, sword and fire.

However formidable the problems raised by the final meeting of Arthur and Guinevere, they pass from the reader's consciousness as soon as the King rides from the convent in answer to the summons of the solitary trumpet:

> . . . more and more
> The moony vapour rolling round the King,
> Who seemed the phantom of a Giant in it,
> Enwound him fold by fold, and made him gray,
> And grayer, till himself became as mist
> Before her, moving ghostlike to his doom.
>
> (G, 596—601)

The role of landscape in giving credence to character is nowhere clearer than in these few lines separating Arthur's distressing words at Almesbury from his speech on the eve of the Last Battle, just before the ghost of Gawain appears in his sleep:

> For I, being simple, thought to work His will,
> And have but stricken with the sword in vain;
> And all whereon I leaned in wife and friend
> Is traitor to my peace, and all my realm
> Reels back into the beast, and is no more.
> My God, thou hast forgotten me in my death:
> Nay—God my Christ—I pass but shall not die.
>
> (PA, 22—28)

Arthur's paraphrase of Christ's last words—"My God, my God, why hast thou forsaken me?"—would have been intolerable if spoken at Almesbury; it is the measure of Tennyson's achievement that in the ghostly context of "The Passing of Arthur" the paraphrase strikes us as neither blasphemous nor fatuous.

In this setting of blighting winds and densest fog,

landscape and dreamscape are so perfectly fused that
Gawain's ghost seems less an intrusion from the supernatural
world than a part of the topography of the Last Battle, which
is itself charged with portents that seem to lift it out of
nature. Gawain has previously appeared in bright
landscapes filled with the pageantry and color of plumed
knights and fair ladies; here he approaches Arthur as a
wailing shadow flitting down the dark corridors of a
windswept dream. Like Dante's carnal sinners helplessly
buffeted by the winds, Gawain, always "light-of-love"
(PE, 353), is "blown / Along a wandering wind." His baser
purposes have failed, as have Arthur's higher purposes, and
so the Gawain of the earlier idylls, ever following the course
of the symbolic season, is here stripped of youth and enters
the dream as the wintry harbinger of Arthur's passing:

> There came on Arthur sleeping, Gawain killed
> In Lancelot's war, the ghost of Gawain blown
> Along a wandering wind, and past his ear
> Went shrilling: "Hollow, hollow all delight!
> Hail, King! tomorrow thou shalt pass away.
> Farewell! there is an isle of rest for thee.
> And I am blown along a wandering wind,
> And hollow, hollow, hollow all delight."
> And fainter onward, like wild birds that change
> Their season in the night and wail their way
> From cloud to cloud, down the long wind the dream
> Shrilled . . .
>
> (30–41)

As Arthur passes from the poem the light associated with
his coming fades into the "blind haze" (76) of the Last
Battle. Three great shafts of light had lit the hall of Camelot
at the coronation and the knights had been dazed as at "the
coming of a light" (CA, 265). On the occasion of Arthur's
arming, the blade of Excalibur shone with blinding brilliance
(CA, 300); his disarming takes place in darkness and friend
slays friend in impenetrable mists. The landscape lapses back

into its aboriginal state, before Arthur cleared the forests
and let in the light:

> Then rose the King and moved his host by night,
> And ever pushed Sir Modred, league by league,
> Back to the sunset bound of Lyonnesse—
> A land of old upheaven from the abyss
> By fire, to sink into the abyss again;
> Where fragments of forgotten peoples dwelt,
> And the long mountains ended in a coast
> Of ever-shifting sand, and far away
> The phantom circle of a moaning sea.
> There the pursuer could pursue no more,
> And he that fled no further fly the King;
> And there, that day when the great light of heaven
> Burned at his lowest in the rolling year,
> On the waste sand by the waste sea they closed.
>
> (79–93)

The bounds of heaven and earth are again obscured, as on
the night of Arthur's birth, and the sinking of the land back
into the abyss foreshadows the instant when all time
will cease. The waning of Arthur's power has become
synonymous with the extinction of human consciousness,
drowned out by the great voice that shakes the waters of
the world and inundates "the narrow realm whereon we
move" (140). Nature is at once formless and fierce, like the
ill-defined shapes locked in confused slaughter:

> Nor ever yet had Arthur fought a fight
> Like this last, dim, weird battle of the west.
> A deathwhite mist slept over sand and sea:
> Whereof the chill, to him who breathed it, drew
> Down with his blood, till all his heart was cold
> With formless fear; and even on Arthur fell
> Confusion, since he saw not whom he fought.
> For friend and foe were shadows in the mist,
> And friend slew friend not knowing whom he slew.
>
> (93–101)

According to his son, Tennyson intended the Last Battle
to represent "A Vision of Death" as well as the overthrow of

the old order.[19] This enigmatic phrase applies with particular
aptness to the closing lines of the battle. The monstrous
oaths and blasphemies of the dying knights echo the climactic
moment in the Apocalypse when, on the field of Armageddon,
"men blasphemed God," islands and mountains were
swallowed up, and the "cities of the nations fell."[20] In this
phantasmic landscape the only sharply defined feature is the
harsh consonantal clash of the words themselves, which
reintroduce into modern English the alliterative stress of
Anglo-Saxon poetry:

> And ever and anon with host to host
> Shocks, and the splintering spear, the hard mail hewn,
> Shield-breakings, and the clash of brands, the crash
> Of battleaxes on shattered helms, and shrieks
> After the Christ, of those who falling down
> Looked up for heaven, and only saw the mist;
> And shouts of heathen and the traitor knights,
> Oaths, insult, filth, and monstrous blasphemies,
> Sweat, writhings, anguish, labouring of the lungs
> In that close mist, and cryings for the light,
> Moans of the dying, and voices of the dead.*
>
> (107–117)

* Cf. the analogous effect a few lines later, when Bedivere carries
Arthur down a narrow pass to the sea. The explosive *b*'s and hard *c*'s
capture the clang of mailed heel on frozen stone, and in the
monosyllabic, alliterative stress—"the bare black cliff clanged"—
one hears something of the bleak strength of *Beowulf*. But once the
narrow descent has been accomplished and the landscape opens
out to the expanse of level water, the verse modulates from the cramped
brevity of hard *c*'s and short *a*'s to the liquid sonorousness of
repeated *l*'s and open *o*'s:

> Dry clashed his harness in the icy caves
> And barren chasms, and all to left and right
> The bare black cliff clanged round him, as he based
> His feet on juts of slippery crag that rang
> Sharp-smitten with the dint of armèd heels—
> And on a sudden, lo! the level lake,
> And the long glories of the winter moon.
>
> (354–360)

Nothing could be further from the languid setting of Isolt's "far-rolling, westward-smiling seas" (LT, 583), and both landscapes are immeasurably removed in time and tone from the Eastertide when Gareth, approaching the distant Camelot, hears the melody of birds on branch and in mid air. Arthur's city built to music falls to the discordant shrieks of men who have reverted to beasts and whose dying cries are echoed by the "phantom circle of a moaning sea."

At the end of the battle a bitter wind blows aside the mist and reveals the totality of the destruction. Nothing stirs except the wan waves, pallid as Arthur in the moonlight, that break over the "dead faces, to and fro / Swaying the helpless hands" (130–131). Bedivere points to a single living figure, Modred, whom Arthur slays. The King's victory over this shadowy negation of himself is even more ambiguous than his victory over the Red Knight, for in destroying Modred he is himself mortally wounded, exactly as he first supplants the heathen and is in turn supplanted by them. Vivien's prophecy that she will beat the Cross to earth and break the King finds its symbolic fulfillment in the ruined chapel—"A broken chancel with a broken cross" (177)—to which Bedivere bears the dying Arthur. There the King commands Bedivere to cast Excalibur into the sea, but before finally doing so he twice betrays the command, wishing to preserve on earth some relic of his lord. The King who once thought men better than they are—Lancelot true—now believes them worse than they are—Bedivere false, a Judas who would "betray me for the precious hilt" (294). To the pathos of Arthur's passing in this "place of tombs" is added the agony of his disillusion, like Christ's at the denial of Peter.

In "The Coming of Arthur" Bleys and Merlin descend a steep chasm down to the sea, where they find the newborn King. In the Round Table idylls the angle of vision at which we view Arthur shifts and he is associated with great heights: Gareth desires to fly up "in ever-highering eagle-circles" to the King, and Merlin has placed a winged statue of Arthur

on the topmost spire of Camelot.[21] In "The Passing of Arthur"
the perspective again reverses itself as Bedivere takes the
King from the chapel and descends the frozen cliffs to the sea.
There the funeral barge arrives to receive him, but the Three
Queens, who stood idly by at the coronation, now have a
narrative function, and as the tallest of the three rests his
bruised head in her lap, we catch the fleeting glimpse of a
pietà. The moans of the dying knights are echoed by the
Queens' "agony of lamentation," which rises like a wind that
blows all night over a wasteland where no man has been
"since the making of the world" (368–371). To this landscape
of primeval desolation Tennyson juxtaposes the island-valley
of Avilion,

> Where falls not hail, or rain, or any snow,
> Nor ever wind blows loudly . . .
>
> (PA, 428–429)

The Queens are to bear Arthur to this "heaven-haven," but
it is an equivocal journey to an equivocal end. Avilion is
beyond time, beyond life, and Arthur's arrival there is as
uncertain as his ultimate return "—if indeed I go / (For all my
mind is clouded with a doubt)—" (425–426). Arthur's last
words from the barge are those of a ghost; he is no longer a
character within the poem but speaks as a kind of final
chorus passing judgment upon the action. Between his first
saying, "The old order changeth, yielding place to new," and
its repetition here, *old* and *new* have reversed their meanings
and it is Arthur's order which yields to the new barbarism.
"The new leaf ever pushes off the old," Vivien had sung in
praise of the old sun-worship, and she has proven at least as
accurate a prophet as Arthur.

With Arthur's embarkation Bedivere remains the last living
figure among the frozen hills. His lament moves us back in
time from the medieval splendors of Camelot to the barren
winterscape of the Anglo-Saxon warrior who outlives his lord

and wanders homeless and liegeless in an alien world, "among new men, strange faces, other minds" (406). Stage by stage Arthur's always insubstantial presence recedes from Bedivere's sight, until he becomes a speck on the faint horizon of the winter dawn. In "The Coming of Arthur" Merlin had said of the King, "From the great deep to the great deep he goes" (410). As Bedivere recalls Merlin's "riddling" words, the reader is in turn reminded that Arthur's departure is also a return, that his passing carries with it the hint of a second coming:

> Then from the dawn it seemed there came, but faint
> As from beyond the limit of the world,
> Like the last echo born of a great cry,
> Sounds, as if some fair city were one voice
> Around a king returning from his wars.
>
> (457–461)

The music first heard at the founding of Camelot is here heard for the last time, but it comes from another world. Arthur has taken his city with him, or rather in again crossing the horizon that separates earth from heaven, he returns disincarnate to the city of his origin. The vanishing barge symbolizes this second transection. In receding from finite space to infinity, Arthur passes beyond time in nature into eternity. Landscape and timescape converge as the King "vanishes into light" (468).

V · Character and Symbol

In his lectures on dreams Freud remarks that "things employed as symbols do not thereby cease to be themselves." [1] All of the characters in the *Idylls* have difficulty in distinguishing between symbols and things, dreams and realities. Alone in her tower, Elaine believes that in possessing Lancelot's shield she possesses Lancelot; a starved symbolist whose waking life no longer nourishes the dream on which she feeds, she dies for a symbol or, in Tennyson's twice-repeated phrase, "lived in fantasy" (LE, 27, 396). Like Arthur, who lives in his "fancy" of the Round Table (LE, 129) and tries to make figs from thistles and men from beasts, Elaine seeks to wrench the intractable world into the shape of her symbols. As her funeral barge vanishes "far-off, a blot upon the stream" (LE, 1381), we catch a foreglimpse of the barge that will bear Arthur to Avilion. Elaine's incapacity to realize her dreams except in death anticipates the larger failure of Arthur to impose his vision upon the world. Yet if Elaine and Arthur die in quest of symbols, Pelleas destroys himself by renouncing them. Men cannot live by symbols, Tennyson seems to be saying, and cannot live without them.

Our most fertile, familiar, yet enigmatic experience of symbols occurs in dreams, whose peculiar economy of connection is mirrored in literature, sacred and secular. The writer has traditionally figured as a dreamer attentively stationed at the entrance to the vision that is his book. Yeats, in his essay "The Symbolism of Poetry," writes of "that state of perhaps real trance, in which the mind liberated from the pressure of will is unfolded in symbols." Yeats describes this state as the midway point between sleep and wakefulness, "the one moment of creation." [2] For Tennyson, too, the waking trance was indispensable not only to his creativity but to his apprehension of reality itself:

A kind of waking trance I have frequently had, quite up from boyhood, when I have been all alone. This has generally come upon me thro' repeating my own name two or three times to myself silently, till all at once, as it were out of the intensity of the consciousness of individuality, the individuality itself seemed to dissolve and fade away into boundless being, and this not a confused state, but the clearest of the clearest . . . utterly beyond words, where death was an almost laughable impossibility, the loss of personality (if so it were) seeming no extinction but the only true life. [3]

At the end of "The Holy Grail" Arthur describes a strikingly similar moment of vision "when he feels he cannot die, / And knows himself no vision to himself" (912–913)—a passage which Tennyson glossed as "the (spiritually) central lines" of the *Idylls*. [4]

Such moments, like the symbols through which they are rendered, are the source of analogies but are never wholly contained by analogy. We know them less by the equivalences they suggest—God as blinding light—than by our conviction that they are charged with a surplus of meaning that overbears comparison. The true symbol always possesses this radical incommensurateness; it does not simply stand for something but half-creates the reality it represents. Carlyle gives us the classic, pre-Freudian definition of the symbol: it reveals "Eternity looking through Time." [5] Like the sacred dove in Christian iconography, the symbol radiates light from the world above upon the world below, and Carlyle traditionally conceives of this effulgence as a downward motion, the

bodying forth of infinite meaning in a finite container. With
the advent of Freud the motion has been reversed. Through
one of those revolutions in consciousness encapsulated in
metaphor, the locus of the real has shifted: the symbol which
once descended from above now rises from below, thrust up
from the subconscious, and its ultimate source is not in Eternity
but in quasi-time, in the mythic racial past.

Yet if symbols now appear to be generated in a different
sphere, they remain the half-magical mediators between our
dreams and waking life, between unconsciousness and
consciousness, nature and supernature, time and eternity.
Arthur Hallam said as much when he exclaimed of Tennyson's
early symbolist poems, in which these divided realms are
fused, "How wonderful the new world thus created for us, the
region between real and unreal!" [6] Tennyson's finest poetry
always originates in "a kind of waking trance" in which the
mind, freed from the inhibitions of will, unfolds itself in
symbols. His persistent use of ambiguity in the *Idylls* is
essentially a defense of the truth of dreams, in which symbol,
setting, and character are alternate manifestations of each
other and an act can be simultaneously good and evil, ecstatic
and terrifying.* Of all literary genres romance is closest to
the wish-fulfillment dream or its counterpart, the thwarted
wish that turns into nightmare. The story of Arthur draws
together these archetypal elements transposed from dreams
—pursuit or perilous journey, quest, combat, ritual death,
and the final recognition or apotheosis of the hero.[7] From this
perspective one can understand the lifelong attraction of a
poet of waking trances to the Arthurian cycle. One

---

* Compare Freud's comment on the "strange tendency" of dreams
"to disregard negation and to express contraries by identical means of
representation." The word "no," Freud contends, "does not seem
to exist for a dream. Dreams show a special tendency to reduce two
opposites to a unity or to represent them as one thing." ("The
Antithetical Sense of Primal Words," *Character and Culture*, ed. Philip
Rieff [New York, Collier Books, 1963], pp. 44–45.)

understands, too, why dreams are so prevalent throughout Tennyson's poetry, and why the *Idylls*, which are so highly charged with symbolism, should be so especially rich in dreams, prophecies, visions, quests, and—most perilous of all such journeys beyond actuality—madness.

Patterned upon the dream, the poem begins with the simple wish-fulfillment of "Gareth and Lynette" and is progressively transformed into the nightmare of the Last Battle. But the transformations, unlike the magical changes in dreams or pure romance, are effected in the context of characters as psychologically convincing as Guinevere or Lancelot, and through motives as operative in waking life as sexual appetite or the drive for political dominion. The dream always hovers just below the surface of the *Idylls*, giving it a surreal intensity. But instead of rejecting the dream element as infantile fantasy, as we might if Vivien literally turned into a serpent, we welcome the subtler mediation of the symbol and find in "lissome Vivien," entwined about the feet of Merlin, the most persuasive embodiment of the Lamia in our literature. Only in "Gareth and Lynette" does Tennyson allow pure wish-fulfillment to dominate the stage, and his reasons for doing so are central to our understanding of the *Idylls*.

"Gareth and Lynette" is by deliberate design what Tennyson's critics have mistaken the whole of the *Idylls* to be—a sheer fairy tale. Although the story employs all the motifs of dream-romance, it is in fact a parody of the form it ostensibly employs. A gutted dream, as it were, the idyll discharges through an undercurrent of burlesque the terrors it factitiously arouses. We feel the characters to be unreal not because they are knights at arms but because they are endowed with no life beyond the literary convention to which they are confined and which Tennyson chooses to undercut. A complex and tragic figure such as Guinevere would be out of place in "Gareth and Lynette," the only idyll in which she is never named or even alluded to. A remark which

Alice Meynell indiscriminately applied to all the characters
of the *Idylls* justly applies to Gareth and Lynette as well as
Geraint and Enid: Tennyson "sheds the luminous sun
of dreams upon men and women who could do well with
footlights." [8] These are the least of the characters in the
Idylls and we regret that Tennyson made no more of them.
But their very deficiency is indispensable to the larger design
of the poem—a romance whose theme is the fatal deficiency
of romance, a fantasy which demands our emancipation
from dreams.

Tennyson's parodic intention in "Gareth and Lynette" is
evident in his modifications of Malory, whose story he
follows in compressed outline but whose tone he everywhere
alters. In Malory as in Tennyson the young knight,
disguised as a knave and in love with a scornful lady,
subdues a series of increasingly fearsome foes, is recognized
to be of noble blood, and wins the lady. But Tennyson
reduces the host of indistinguishable adversaries in Malory
to four brothers, each emblematic of a stage of life, and
through Gareth's mock-heroic encounters with these
grotesquely costumed, allegorical brethren he tips the balance
of the tale from romance to burlesque.* "These four, / Who

---

* Cf., for example, the savage combat between Beaumains and the two
brothers in the *Morte d'Arthur* (bk. VII, ch. 6) with its mock-heroic
counterpart in the *Idylls*. Gareth encounters the huge, red-faced
Knight of the Noonday Sun in midstream: " 'Ugh!' cried the Sun, and
vizoring up a red / And cipher face of rounded foolishness, / Pushed
horse across the foamings of the ford" (1012–1014). They exchange
four blows,

but as the Sun
Heaved up a ponderous arm to strike the fifth,
The hoof of his horse slipt in the stream, the stream
Descended, and the Sun was washed away.

(1018–1021)

Much later in the *Idylls* Pelleas, also in disguise and dressed in
"blood-red armour," rides down upon Arthur and tumbles, sodden,
into the water, where his face is trampled into slime. The parallelism
in setting is as striking as the difference in effect. A hint of parody

be they?" Arthur asks Lynette, who replies, "They be of foolish fashion, O Sir King, / The fashion of that old knight-errantry" (611–614). And in lines that Tennyson surely intended as the key to the entire idyll, Lynette describes a hermit's cave with figures of ancient knights sculptured on the walls:

> . . . a hermit once was here,
> Whose holy hand hath fashioned on the rock
> The war of Time against the soul of man.
> And yon four fools have sucked their allegory
> From these damp walls, and taken but the form.
>   (1166–1170)

The passage hints at a far greater allegory that, according to tradition, was also recorded by a holy man in a cave— Saint John on Patmos, whose Four Horsemen of the Apocalypse are bizarrely mimicked by Gareth's four adversaries.[9] The defeat of human aspiration in the face of time is the substance of the *Idylls*, but only its mocking shadow plays over "Gareth and Lynette." And so Tennyson gives us "but the form," cardboard characters in a medieval charade.

In a rapid reading of "Gareth and Lynette" the burlesque element rarely rises to the surface. One is still under the spell of "The Coming of Arthur," and the crucial lines describing Gareth's first sight of Camelot (which have no precedent in Malory) overshadow the "fool's parable" (979) of the four brothers. The Camelot passage states in earnest the theme of the elusiveness of reality that is handled lightly

---

may also be detected in the arming of the Knight of the Evening Star. In place of the Lady of the Lake, who presents Arthur with Excalibur in "The Coming," a grizzled woman arms the Evening Star, who is encased in the hardened skins of animals. At this stage in the *Idylls* men *affect* a bestiality which comes to them unnaturally; later, the disguise becomes the reality, the human dress a mere mask.

elsewhere in "Gareth and Lynette." Admittedly, the mixing
of genres can have effects as dismal as the mixing of drinks,
and a certain overhang of the amateur theatrical, of which
the Victorians were so fond, mars "Gareth and Lynette,"
just as traces of the domestic idyll mar the story of Geraint
and Enid.

Yet in "Gareth and Lynette" Tennyson succeeds in using
an intentionally inferior fiction to lend contrasting weight to
the far profounder fiction of "Pelleas and Ettarre." Again,
his departures from Malory highlight his intention. In
Tennyson as in Malory, Pelleas is an infatuated knight in love
with a scornful lady, and in both versions the false Gawain
is discovered sleeping with Ettarre. But Tennyson radically
changes the end of the tale. In Malory, Pelleas enlists the aid
of Nimue, who breaks the spell of his infatuation, and the
two spend the rest of their days making love. Malory in
effect tells the tale of Gareth and Lynette all over again, and
we remain locked in the timeless, untroubled world of
romance.[10] Tennyson heightens the make-believe quality of
"Gareth and Lynette" in order to turn its counterpart,
"Pelleas and Ettarre," into a potent anti-romance. "Gareth
and Lynette" marks the Edenic phase of Camelot, "Pelleas
and Ettarre" marks the Fall, and everything that follows it,
the Expulsion.

With the shift from romance to tragedy, character emerges
from the confines of type and acquires a psychological
reality subject to the necessities of a mutable world. Unlike
Gareth and Lynette, Pelleas and Ettarre, whatever else they
may symbolize, "do not thereby cease to be themselves."
Indeed, it is perhaps the most striking fact about the *Idylls*
that through the interweaving of character and landscape,
story and symbol, the men and women of the poem take on
an enhanced individuality, a vital interaction among
themselves and their settings that lends reality to the castles
and meadows through which they move.

Of all the characters in the *Idylls* Pelleas suffers the
bitterest fate, for although he loses his innocence he never
achieves wisdom, but merely substitutes one illusion for its
opposite. Once he believed that everything appearing fair
was in fact so; after he rides in shock from Ettarre's garden
he says of himself and the sleeping lovers,

> Fool, beast—he, she, or I? myself most fool;
> Beast too, as lacking human wit—disgraced,
> Dishonoured all for trial of true love—
> Love?—we be all alike: only the King
> Hath made us fools and liars. O noble vows!
> O great and sane and simple race of brutes
> That own no lust because they have no law!*
> (466–472)

The closing lines of the idyll dramatize through the deftest
of juxtapositions that even the fallen are not all alike, that
Guinevere's garden is not Ettarre's. The maddened Pelleas
comes upon Lancelot, who is "warm with a gracious parting
from the Queen" (547). Pelleas swears to publicize their
crime throughout the kingdom, attacks Lancelot, and falls
unhorsed to the ground. "Thou art false as Hell: slay me,"
Pelleas shrieks, to which Lancelot magnanimously replies,
"Rise, weakling; I am Lancelot; say thy say" (564, 570).
Pelleas has equated the treachery of Gawain and Ettarre with
that of Lancelot and Guinevere, but as the aging Lancelot
spares the boy-knight's life, we are made to feel the
difference, as we are again compelled to do in the final scene,
when the Queen graciously addresses the mute and shattered
Pelleas:

---

* Pelleas' last line alludes to Paul's Epistle to the Romans:
"Where no law is, there is no transgression . . . I had not known sin,
but by the law: for I had not known lust, except the law had said,
Thou shalt not covet" (4:15; 7:7). Pelleas' use of the Bible suggests
that Tennyson took seriously the belief that even the Devil can
cite Scripture. Significantly, it is only *after* Pelleas becomes Arthur's
adversary, and hence a type of Antichrist, that he quotes the Bible, thus
joining the company of Mark, Modred, and Vivien.

"O young knight,
Hath the great heart of knighthood in thee failed
So far thou canst not bide, unfrowardly,
A fall from *him?*" Then, for he answered not,
"Or hast thou other griefs? If I, the Queen,
May help them, loose thy tongue, and let me know."
(583–588)

Burdened as they are by time and guilt, Lancelot and
Guinevere are nowhere nobler than in this scene. Yet theirs
is a flawed nobility, far more catastrophic in its consequences
to the realm than the meaner treachery of Gawain and
Ettarre. And if Tennyson here emphasizes their nobility,
as he later does through a similar juxtaposition with Tristram
and Isolt, he offers them no easy absolution. As the Queen
looks "hard upon her lover, he on her" (592), Modred
spies them both and knows the time is hard at hand.

Throughout the *Idylls* one is struck by how frequently
erotic obsession is the motive force of action. It is self-evident
in Pelleas' misplaced passion for Ettarre, in Geraint's
uxorious worship of Enid, Gareth's infatuation with Lynette,
Elaine's with Lancelot, and Merlin's with Vivien. It binds
the wavering Tristram to Isolt and links all of their separate
tales to the overriding love of Lancelot and Guinevere. One
finds it, too, where it is least expected, in Arthur, for
example, or in Percivale's sister, the holy nun whose vision
of the Grail sends the knights on their disastrous quest.
Incapacity for such obsession is the distinguishing quality
of the three characters who dedicate themselves to destroying
the kingdom: Mark, Modred, and Vivien. A frigid stealth
characterizes the first two, and Vivien, herself a dazzling
sexual object, is conspicuously free of the passion she
arouses in others.

Arthur's first sight of Guinevere has as shattering and
lasting an effect upon him as the first sight of Lancelot has
upon Guinevere. Arthur "felt the light of her eyes into his
life / Smite on the sudden" (CA, 56–57), and we are given
no evidence whatsoever to doubt the truth of his marriage

vow—"I love thee to the death!"—words he sees fit to echo
as he rides from Almesbury to his doom: "I love thee still"
(CA, 467; G, 556). The failure of his marriage leads
directly to the moral fragmentation of the kingdom and to
the temper of spiritual desperation that inspires the Grail
quest. The nun whose vision sets the quest in motion recalls
Elaine, except that her thwarted erotic passion fulfills itself
in religious ecstasy rather than death.[11] She is a *femme fatale*
turned *religieuse*, and the scene in which she persuades
Galahad to seek the Grail is a mixture of incantation and
betrothal. "My knight, my love, my knight of heaven," she
addresses him, "I, maiden, round thee, maiden, bind my
belt" (157–159). A beneficent Vivien, she weaves a spell of
words around the enthralled Galahad. "Go forth," she urges,

> "till one will crown thee king
> Far in the spiritual city:" and as she spake
> She sent the deathless passion in her eyes
> Through him, and made him hers, and laid her mind
> On him, and he believed in her belief.
> (HG, 160–165)

It is one of the more daring ironies of the *Idylls* that the
holy nun is as responsible for the Round Table's loss of
Galahad as the harlot Vivien is for the loss of Merlin.

Vivien is a female anti-Arthur at once brighter and far
more dangerous than Pelleas. Her single-minded aim of
destroying the kingdom endows her with a nihilistic
exuberance that contrasts with the divided, melancholic wills
of those on whom she preys. She lies with the ease, swift
inventiveness, and fertile circumstantiality of all gifted liars.
The words she imputes to Guinevere of Lancelot—"Rise, my
sweet King, and kiss me on the lips, / Thou art my King"
(BB, 508–509)—have the regal ring of the Queen and suffice
to undo Balin, who serves as her trial run for the more
formidable undoing of Merlin.

Vivien's boy-squire raises the visors of the fallen Balin
and Balan as she exclaims,

> "Goodly!—look!
> They might have cropt the myriad flower of May,
> And butt each other here, like brainless bulls,
> Dead for one heifer!"
>
> (BB, 566–569)

Only Vivien could have compared the Queen to a heifer,
just as she characterizes Arthur's knights as bulls, fools, and
swine. Yet despite her quick intelligence Vivien, too, is
subject to delusion and assumes the motive of the fratricide
to have been sexual rivalry.[12] Her perversity, which she has
learned, literally, from the hands of Mark, is finely suggested
by the contrast between the close of "Balin and Balan" and
the opening of "Merlin and Vivien": in the one we see
her toying with the boy-squire; in the other she makes love
to the ancient sage.

Of all the idylls, "Merlin and Vivien" was most coldly
received by Tennyson's contemporaries. The reviewer for
Blackwood's deplored Tennyson's having "pollute[d] the
pages which tell, further on, of the manly—, ay, the *Christian*
—purity of Arthur." [13] And Swinburne seized the occasion
to berate Tennyson for depicting "the erotic fluctuations
and vacillations of a dotard under the moral and physical
manipulation of a prostitute." [14] But as there is nothing crude,
so there is nothing prudish in Tennyson's story of an old
man's erotic surrender to a brilliant harlot. For his plot
Tennyson takes virtually nothing from the *Morte d'Arthur*,
in which the fall of Merlin is a minor, one-page episode:
Merlin in his dotage becomes "assotted upon" Vivien and
"always . . . lay about the lady to have her maidenhood." To
escape his lecherous assaults Vivien enchants him, leaving
him forever stuck under a stone.[15] In place of Malory's
doting magician and innocent damsel, Tennyson creates the
great figure of the harlot-enchantress, a worthy adversary
of the Merlin who knows the range of all the arts and built
the King's havens, ships, and halls. The result is that Merlin
is doomed but not degraded by Vivien, and his fall, a

peripheral episode in Malory, is made central to the fall of
the Round Table.

Vivien cannot bring about that fall by attacking Arthur
directly, for he is invulnerable to her charms, indeed unaware
of them, an obliviousness that in another context causes
Guinevere to condemn him as a "moral child" (LE, 145).
Once Vivien tries to seduce Arthur, but the attempt is
half-hearted because the intended result so unlikely. Arthur
walks by her blankly, and it makes "the laughter of an
afternoon / That Vivien should attempt the blameless King"
(MV, 161–162). But she can work her will indirectly,
through Merlin, who embodies the ancient fusion of magic
and wisdom that has built the realm. There is a peculiar
aptness, like that of blood-kin unwittingly drawn together
in some Greek myth, in the encounter of the young sorceress
and the ancient sage. Both wizard and witch are ages older
than the fragile new experiment in civilization that Camelot
represents. Vivien's lust for Merlin is feigned only in its
carnality, not its intensity, for it is his mind and not his body
that she is driven to possess. He wields his white magic
for good; she wields her sex magic for evil and is attracted
to Merlin as strongly as Iago to Othello or Claggart to
Billy Budd. Her need for Merlin goes deeper even than the
need for sex; it is the need to soil and destroy, and shows
itself in her attitude toward death, by which she is at once
fascinated and horrified, as befits her birth among corpses.
Mark goads her into subverting Camelot by accusing her of
fearing the "monkish manhood" of Arthur's knights, to
which she replies:

"Why fear? because that fostered at *thy* court
I savour of thy—virtues? fear them? no.
As Love, if Love be perfect, casts out fear,
So Hate, if Hate be perfect, casts out fear.
My father died in battle against the King,
My mother on his corpse in open field;
She bore me there, for born from death was I

Among the dead and sown upon the wind—
And then on thee! and shown the truth betimes,
That old true filth, and bottom of the well,
Where Truth is hidden."

(38–48)

Vivien is a philosopher as well as a student of Scripture,
which she quotes to better effect than anyone else in the
Idylls. Fittingly, she defines herself in an inverted paraphrase
of the First Epistle of John: "There is no fear in love; but
perfect love casteth out fear."[16] Like Satan and Sin, whose
incestuous union begets Death in *Paradise Lost*, Vivien is
born of rebellion and death ("My father died in battle against
the King"), and begets them both throughout the *Idylls*.
The begetting is of course figurative, for Vivien, "sown
upon the wind" and then upon Mark, is sterile: "For they
have sown the wind, and they shall reap the whirlwind . . .
the bud shall yield no meal."[17] The only character in the
Idylls to understand Mark perfectly, Vivien hates him with
that perfect hatred which is her closest approximation to love.
"Well, I loved thee first," she says; "that warps the wit"
(60–61).

Tennyson added the opening scene at Mark's court long
after the first publication of "Merlin and Vivien." The
interpolation prepares the reader for Mark's climactic role in
"The Last Tournament" and, more to our present purpose,
gives to Vivien a depth of characterization she had previously
lacked. A final addition, brief but crucial, points up Merlin's
peculiar vulnerability prior to the seduction and links his
fall to the impending fall of the realm:

Then fell on Merlin a great melancholy;
He walked with dreams and darkness, and he found
A doom that ever poised itself to fall,
An ever-moaning battle in the mist,
World-war of dying flesh against the life,
Death in all life and lying in all love,

The meanest having power upon the highest,
And the high purpose broken by the worm.

(187–194)

"Merlin and Vivien" dramatizes Vivien's prophecy in
"Balin and Balan" that she will beat the Cross to earth and
break the King. Although Merlin knows that Arthur's high
purpose will be broken by the worm, his very foreknowledge
serves to incapacitate him, even when—perhaps especially
when—the worm entwines itself about him in the form of
the serpent-temptress Vivien:

"Great Master, do ye love me?" he was mute.
And lissome Vivien, holding by his heel,
Writhed toward him, slided up his knee and sat,
Behind his ankle twined her hollow feet
Together, curved an arm about his neck,
Clung like a snake . . .

(235–240)

Vivien here combines the roles of Eve and Satan. She lusts
for Merlin's forbidden knowledge and in grasping his heel,
like the serpent in Genesis who bruises man's heel, she brings
death into the world.[18] Her affinity with death is especially
marked later in the idyll, when Merlin summons the last of
his failing powers of resistance and repulses her with the
epithet "harlot." The ironically-named *Vivien* (*vivus*:
alive) leaps from his lap "stiff as a viper frozen" and her face
momentarily reveals "the bare-grinning skeleton of death"
(843–845). An incarnate symbol, Vivien revitalizes the
outworn literary convention from which she derives. The
femme fatale who makes her appearance in Keats's "La Belle
Dame Sans Merci" achieves her most potent realization
in Vivien and by the end of the century dwindles into a
figure of sado-masochist jest.

Psychologically one of the subtlest of the idylls,
narratively "Merlin and Vivien" is the simplest. The entire
action centers on the two protagonists and the single event
foreseen in the opening line—"A storm was coming, but

the winds were still"—and consummated in the tempest
which bursts at its close. What Vivien has failed to achieve
by art she does by nature; her terror at the "livid-flickering
fork" of lightning (939) sends her helpless into the arms of
Merlin, whose pale blood takes on at her touch "gayer
colours, like an opal warmed" (948). The moaning storm
and the silent actors take on a kind of expressionist
interanimation. The climax of the storm marks the sexual
climax of Merlin, which occurs as the rotten branch snaps
overhead and the glittering, serpentine body of Vivien
"went and came":

>   . . . and ever overhead
> Bellowed the tempest, and the rotten branch
> Snapt in the rushing of the river-rain
> Above them; and in change of glare and gloom
> Her eyes and neck glittering went and came;
> Till now the storm, its burst of passion spent,
> Moaning and calling out of other lands,
> Had left the ravaged woodland yet once more
> To peace; and what should not have been had been,
> For Merlin, overtalked and overworn,
> Had yielded, told her all the charm, and slept.
>   (954–964)

The idyll ends with Vivien's exultant cry over Merlin,
"O fool!"—which the forest closing about her echoes as she
rides away. The reiterated epithet is apt, for Merlin, once
all mind—Arthur's wizard, counselor, architect, and bard—
is now a mute and impotent fool.

The narrative simplicity of "Merlin and Vivien" contrasts
with the extreme intricacy of the plotting in "The Last
Tournament." All of the action in the latter idyll concentrates
our awareness upon the juxtaposed sets of adulterous
triangles: Arthur-Guinevere-Lancelot and Mark-Isolt-
Tristram. Tennyson achieved a similar effect in "Pelleas and
Ettarre" by linking the treachery of Gawain and Ettarre to
that of Lancelot and Guinevere. But there his chief concern

was with the disintegration of Pelleas; here, it is with the disintegration of the whole kingdom and the strange salvage cast up from the wreckage, the transfiguration of Lancelot and Guinevere.

From Gottfried von Strassburg through Richard Wagner the Tristan myth has remained the supreme exaltation of romantic love in Western literature. Tennyson, writing at the same time as Wagner, gives us the anti-Wagnerian version of the legend, exactly as Shakespeare in *Troilus and Cressida* subverts the story of Chaucer's lovers, denuding it of romance and setting it against the chill background of a collapsing civilization. The key to Tennyson's intention is the conspicuous absence from the *Idylls* of the love potion. His Tristram and Isolt experience not the raptures of transcendent passion but the withdrawal of all transcendence that leads the late-arriving Tristram to swear "but by the shell" (270) and Isolt to crave lies she can suck "like sweet wines" (640). What Tennyson takes from Tristram and Isolt he gives to Lancelot and Guinevere; the love potion the former never taste becomes that fatal first meeting of Lancelot and Guinevere, which Tennyson never allows them or the reader to forget.*

---

* A note of Tennyson's on "The Last Tournament" makes it clear that he intended the transference: "Tristram had told his uncle Mark of the beauty of Isolt, when he saw her in Ireland, so Mark demanded her hand in marriage, which he obtained. Then Mark sent Tristram to fetch her *as in my Idylls Arthur sent Lancelot for Guinevere*" (Cited in Christopher Ricks, ed., *The Poems of Tennyson* [London, Longmans, 1969], p. 1719; italics added.) The fetching is first described in "The Coming of Arthur" (446–451) and then recalled in "Balin and Balan" (265–269), "Merlin and Vivien" (133–134, 772–775), and "Guinevere" (375–397). Tennyson realized that the design of the *Idylls* compelled him to do less than justice to the Tristan legend. According to Hallam Tennyson, one of his father's unrealized ambitions in later years was to weave "'into a great stage drama the legend of 'Tristram of Lyonnesse' which he had been obliged to cut down so as to suit his treatment of the 'Idylls of the King.'" (*Materials for a Life of A. T.* [privately published, 1895], IV, 242n1.)

The two triangles draw together early in "The Last Tournament," when Lancelot presents Tristram with the prize of "dead innocence." Offended by the craven lawlessness of the tournament and longing to shake off the "burthen of his heart" in death, Lancelot tauntingly asks Tristram, "Hast thou won? / Art thou the purest, brother?" (191–192). Tristram resents the grudging presentation of the prize and replies,

> O chief knight,
> Right arm of Arthur in the battlefield,
> Great brother, thou nor I have made the world;
> Be happy in thy fair Queen as I in mine.
>
> (201–204)

"Great brother" is both taunt and tribute to a fellow adulterer. Under Arthur's aegis Lancelot has in fact "made the world," now sees it being unmade before his eyes, and holds himself responsible for the unmaking. For Tristram, who came after the heathen wars were over, that earlier world is irretrievably remote, and in going to Tintagil he abandons it altogether. He is a modern Lancelot, as Isolt is a younger Guinevere whose suffering renders her not tragic but neurotic.

Tristram's will is incapable of settling on any fixed object, and as he wanders through the woods, vacillating in his reverie between Isolt his mistress and Isolt his wife, the slightest movement is capable of distracting him.[19] "I know not what I would," he says (497), and Isolt, "plucked one way" by her hate of Mark and another by her love of Tristram, is "drained of her force" (537–538). Tristram's alienation from the ideals of the Round Table severs him from the Arthurian past, which he dismisses as a noble fiction, and from all commitment to the future. His entire consciousness is immersed in the flux of the present, as epitomized by his song in praise of new love to suit the newer day. He is a celebrant not only of the new naturalism but of a new sense of time in which the self, insofar as it achieves any definition

at all, is defined only by its ever-shifting experience. The
forest through which he rides, alert as a beast of prey but with
none of its fixity of purpose, is an image of his acute
animal consciousness. Isolt accuses him of growing to
resemble the wild beasts that he hunts, an accusation justified
by his bestial rebuff of the enigmatic woman he meets
weeping beside a cross (492–505). "Why weep ye?"
Tristram asks; "Lord," she replies, "my man / Hath left me
or is dead." To which Tristram retorts,

> "Yet weep not thou, lest, if thy mate return,
> He find thy favour changed and love thee not,"

and rides off as Mark's hounds bellow ominously in the
distance. The reader, too, hears echoes, but of another sort.
In the Gospel of John, Mary Magdalene stands beside the
empty tomb: "Why weepest thou?" the angels ask, and Mary
answers, "Because they have taken away my Lord" (20:13).
The woman whom Tristram taunts beside the cross is clearly
emblematic of Mary, but whereas Tristram cynically casts
doubt upon the return of her Lord, Mary is rewarded by the
return of Jesus, risen in Glory. Tristram's mocking inversion
of the Gospels is the prelude to his fall.

Tennyson places Tristram and Isolt outside all social
necessity and beyond all ties except those to each other.
Hence Tristram boasts that his love is so great because it is
"not bounded save by love" (699). Yet this very
boundlessness is its fatal limitation. Lacking innocence
and incapable of remorse, they renounce the burden of guilt
that finally saves Lancelot and Guinevere and moves us to
forgive them to the degree that they refuse to forgive
themselves. Nothing could more dramatically mark
Tennyson's anti-Wagnerian intention than the brutal
abruptness of the "love-death music" in "The Last
Tournament." Tristram, about to place the carcanet around
Isolt's neck, hungers equally for her and for food, giving her

a last lie to suck before he gratifies both appetites. Touching
"the warm white apple of her throat," he says,

"Press this a little closer, sweet, until—
Come, I am hungered and half-angered—meat,
Wine, wine—and I will love thee to the death,
And out beyond into the dream to come."
. . .
But, while he bowed to kiss the jewelled throat,
Out of the dark, just as the lips had touched,
Behind him rose a shadow and a shriek—
"Mark's way," said Mark, and clove him through the brain.*
(712–715, 745–748)

The idyll closes with Dagonet huddled at Arthur's feet,
a reminder of Vivien at Merlin's feet and a foreglimpse of
Guinevere cringing at Arthur's. The last recruit to the
disintegrating Round Table, Dagonet is, fittingly, a fool. He
is a bit of wreckage washed up from Lear's world onto the
shores of Lyonnesse, and it is appropriate that even in this
world of archaisms he should be faintly archaic. For he
embodies a traditional order of social loyalties at a time when
the privacies of Tristram's new life and new love represent

---

* Up to this moment we (like Tristram and Isolt) are unaware of
Mark's presence at Tintagil. But with this line we realize that he has
all along been stalking the lovers and has overheard Isolt's earlier
reference to "Mark's way to steal behind one in the dark." (613;
cf. 514: "Catlike through his own castle steals my Mark.") Mark,
like Modred, is sinister even in his absences. His final act of
malevolent stealth is in perfect keeping with his entry into the poem in
"Gareth and Lynette." There, appearing indirectly, he dispatches a
messenger to Camelot with a cloth of gold to bribe Arthur into
granting him knighthood. Arthur spurns the gift from the "craven"
Mark—"a man of plots, / Craft, poisonous counsels, wayside
ambushings"—and hints at Mark's future action by describing him as
one "who strikes nor lets the hand be seen" (423–427). In "Balin
and Balan" Mark again appears only by indirection, when the
woodland music is silenced by Vivien, who comes "from out the hall
of Mark" (431), and who draws Mark's portrait more fully in the
crucial flashback at the start of "Merlin and Vivien." Much of Mark's
sinister strength stems from Tennyson's skill in holding him back

the only "rational" adjustment to a fragmented world. The Fool himself knows this and calls Arthur a fool for trying to make "figs out of thistles . . . / And men from beasts" (356–358). Yet if Arthur is a fool, he is a fool of God, as Dagonet implies by his allusion to Christ's words,[20] and such folly may be wiser than the wisdom of men. Hence Dagonet's ironic affirmation: "Long live the king of fools!" (358)

Dagonet's great speech about the "dirty nurse, Experience" marks the immense distance we have traveled from the Founding, with its sense of a newly created world, to the Last Tournament. The whole middle range of humanity which had gathered and formed itself around Arthur— Guinevere, Lancelot, Gareth, Gawain, Balin, Percivale, Pelleas —has dispersed or died, leaving only the Fool, the King, and his adversary Modred. Dagonet, who had been "smuttier than blasted grain" before joining Arthur, reverses the predominant movement in the poem by reeling back, as it

---

from all *present* action in the poem until his actual appearance in "The Last Tournament," when he speaks only two words and his single act defines him with perfect and appalling economy. Tennyson's achievement is the more remarkable when we recall the long, irregular composition of the *Idylls*. As Kathleen Tillotson points out, Mark did not appear at all in the original version of "Merlin and Vivien" and the contemporary reader of the Idylls did not meet him until 1871 in "The Last Tournament." ("Tennyson's Serial Poem," *Mid-Victorian Studies* [London, University of London, Athlone Press, 1965], p. 105.)

Modred is even more taciturn than Mark. His brother Gareth describes him during their childhood as "mute," "sullen," and "biting his thin lips" (GL, 31–32), a characterization that holds throughout the *Idylls*. Although Modred figures in twenty separate scenes, he speaks in only two, once in secret to himself—"And Modred thought, 'The time is hard at hand'" (PE, 597)—and once in a flashback, when in his one and only line of dialogue he betrays Lancelot and Guinevere at their parting interview (G, 105). In the climactic action of the poem, when he mortally wounds Arthur, he is totally silent, and he dies without uttering a word.

were, into the man. Being a fool, he rises too late; being wise, he chooses Arthur's illusions over Tristram's "philosophies":

> "I have wallowed, I have washed—the world
> Is flesh and shadow—I have had my day.
> The dirty nurse, Experience, in her kind
> Hath fouled me—an I wallowed, then I washed—
> I have had my day and my philosophies—
> And thank the Lord I am King Arthur's fool."
>
> (315–320)

With the end of "The Last Tournament" Arthur again becomes the dominant figure in the poem, as he was at its beginning. The whole design of the *Idylls* demands that, as there can be no tournaments after the Last Tournament, so there can be no poem after Arthur's passing. If this seems self-evident, the obviousness is a tribute to Tennyson's architectonics, for Malory ends the *Morte* not with the death of Arthur but with the penitence and deaths of Lancelot and Guinevere.[21] In closing the *Idylls* with Arthur's death, Tennyson has to work the parting and repentance of Lancelot and Guinevere into the earlier narrative and, more difficult, he must make convincing those strains which even at the height of their love lead to their separation.

This he does early in "Balin and Balan," when Lancelot pauses between the paths of lilies and roses and Guinevere chides his hesitancy with that regal sensuality and self-possession she retains almost to the end. In "Lancelot and Elaine" the lovers move to the center of the poem, with Lancelot torn between the lily of Elaine and the rose of Guinevere. The idyll is a study in shattered illusions and broken trusts, symbolized by the diamonds that are won by Lancelot, slip in dreams from Elaine's hands, pass perfidiously through Gawain's, and are flung in rage from Guinevere's. Elaine loves with obsessive fidelity the "falsely true" Lancelot, who half loves her but remains true to the adulterous Guinevere, who mistakenly believes him false.

Two lines of Elizabethan oxymoron epitomize the ironies of Lancelot's dilemma:

> His honour rooted in dishonour stood,
> And faith unfaithful kept him falsely true.
>
> (871–872)

Perhaps too ornate for our taste, the style of "Lancelot and Elaine" is intentionally artificial. Guinevere is "the flower of all the west and all the world," Lancelot "the darling of the court, / Loved of the loveliest" (248, 260–261). But their courtly grace masks a moral decadence, a worm within the rose that Tennyson deftly suggests through an overelaborateness of language. In this world in which courtesy is a mere form and corruption the substance, the inflated style functions as a vehicle of moral judgment. Arthur commissions Gawain to bring the diamond to the wounded Lancelot, but Gawain with his accustomed courtesy— "Courtesy with a touch of traitor in it" (635)—betrays his mission and attempts to seduce Elaine. As Gawain places the prize in Elaine's hand, his parting is a jarring blend of the tritely florid and the cynically prosaic ("a diamond is a diamond"):

> "For if you love, it will be sweet to give it;
> And if he love, it will be sweet to have it
> From your own hand; and whether he love or not,
> A diamond is a diamond. Fare you well
> A thousand times!—a thousand times farewell!"
>
> (688–692)

The fancier turns of speech in "Lancelot and Elaine" are likely to blind the modern reader to the dramatic directness of Guinevere or the naive simplicity of Elaine. Guinevere, for example, enjoins Lancelot, "I pray you: have your joys apart" (1210). And Elaine speaks in a style appropriate to a lily-maid who lives in fantasy, composes her own love-death music, stages her own funeral, and dies in the delusion that

she has loved "one peerless, without stain."[22] To the
innocent voice of Elaine, Tennyson contrasts the tense,
mature intonation of the guilt-ridden Guinevere. She retains
her superb regality, agreeing to receive Lancelot "With such
and so unmoved a majesty / She might have seemed her
statue" (1164–1165); but the rage beneath her composure
rises to the surface when the oblivious Arthur tells her the
"good news" that Lancelot was seen wearing the token of a
lady and may end his bachelorhood:

> "Yea, lord," she said,
> "Thy hopes are mine," and saying that, she choked,
> And sharply turned about to hide her face,
> Past to her chamber, and there flung herself
> Down on the great King's couch, and writhed upon it,
> And clenched her fingers till they bit the palm,
> And shrieked out "Traitor!" to the unhearing wall.
> (602–608)

In Guinevere's eyes, Arthur's very unawareness of her
adultery is itself a cause of the adultery. Her logic is at fault
but the order of her reproaches is psychologically perfect:

> "He never spake word of reproach to me,
> He never had a glimpse of mine untruth,
> He cares not for me."
> (124–126)

Tortured by her own guilt and her presumption of Lancelot's
perfidy, she cannot bear Arthur's "passionate perfection"
(122) and, herself a moral truant, concludes that Arthur is
"A moral child without the craft to rule, / Else had he not
lost me" (145–146). Guinevere is of course right, as is
Dagonet in calling Arthur a fool; yet as the *Idylls* everywhere
compels us to see, in sharing their judgment we are also
judging ourselves and the fallen world.

Elaine's idealism cannot survive the tainted court and she
escapes into death. She remains a figure of romance, unlike

Guinevere and Lancelot, who make the agonized transition from romance to actuality. Lancelot's arms are "battle-writhen"; compared to Elaine's, Guinevere's are "haggard" (807, 1220). With growing fatality they begin to talk of their love in the past tense: ". . . that summer, when ye loved me first" (104). Guinevere's very need to rationalize her adultery attests to her increasing uncertainty about Lancelot and herself.

In Lancelot self-doubt has grown much deeper, for he has assumed the burden of guilt that Guinevere still defers. Her dominant emotion is controlled rage; his is a baffled mixture of self-contempt and contempt for the world. Rejecting the innocent Elaine and irreconciled to his guilty love of Guinevere, Lancelot at the end of the idyll is the most solitary of Arthur's knights, wifeless, heirless, alien even to himself:

> "For what am I? what profits me my name
> Of greatest knight? I fought for it, and have it:
> Pleasure to have it, none; to lose it, pain;
> Now grown a part of me: but what use in it?
> To make men worse by making my sin known?
> Or sin seem less, the sinner seeming great?"
> (1402–1407)

He half nerves himself to break his bonds with Guinevere, but adds at once, "not without / She wills it," and compounds his uncertainty by wondering, "would I, if she willed it?" (1409–1411). Lancelot's deference to Guinevere's will goes much deeper than the conventions of courtly love; despite his strength in battle, he is weaker than she in love because he is far more divided in will.[23]

Increasingly Lancelot is beset by a sense of entrapment, as if he were as much a tragic victim of the evil that rends the kingdom as one of its agents. Lancelot is Arthur's "right arm" and the usurper of Arthur's bed; more than any other of the knights he personifies Arthur's vision of life, and more than any other he shatters that vision. The conflict of contending elements within Lancelot is as fierce as the civil war that destroys the realm, and Tennyson appropriately links the two struggles through the imagery of warfare:

> The great and guilty love he bare the Queen
> In battle with the love he bare his lord,
> Had marred his face, and marked it ere his time.
> (244–246)

The warfare has marred his mind as well; another man "sinning on such heights" would have been

> the sleeker for it; but in him
> His mood was often like a fiend, and rose
> And drove him into wastes and solitudes.
> (249–251)

Lancelot's madness in the wasteland is prophetic of the universal madness which overtakes the Round Table in "The Holy Grail" and which, although it destroys the kingdom, leads to his salvation. The last two lines of "Lancelot and Elaine" serve as prologue to his final act in Lancelot's moral drama:

> So groaned Sir Lancelot in remorseful pain,
> Not knowing he should die a holy man.

Tennyson reserves the climactic position in "The Holy Grail" for Lancelot's account of his quest, for as he is the divided hero of the love story in "Lancelot and Elaine," so he is a failed saint in the spiritual quest for the Grail. He dominates the great middle ground of the poem, standing midway between Galahad, who effortlessly achieves the quest, and Gawain, who, "too blind to have desire to see" (HG, 868), effortlessly evades it. Lancelot desperately desires to see but at the end of his quest is half-blinded by a burning light:

"Then in my madness I essayed the door;
It gave; and through a stormy glare, a heat
As from a seventimes-heated furnace,[24] I,
Blasted and burnt, and blinded as I was,
With such a fierceness that I swooned away—
O, yet methought I saw the Holy Grail,

            . . .

And but for all my madness and my sin,
And then my swooning, I had sworn I saw
That which I saw; but what I saw was veiled . . .
                          (838–843, 846–848)

The equivocal nature of Lancelot's vision accords with his
own mixed condition, which combines all that is exemplary
with much that is flawed in the Round Table. His confession
of failure reflects a keen awareness of this condition and
recalls that inextricable fusion of greatness and guilt which
distinguishes him in "Lancelot and Elaine":

            . . . "in me lived a sin
So strange, of such a kind, that all of pure,
Noble, and knightly in me twined and clung
Round that one sin, until the wholesome flower
And poisonous grew together, each as each,
Not to be plucked asunder."
                          (HG, 769–774)

Lancelot's metaphor of the entwined flowers echoes back to
the garden scene in "Balin and Balan," to the lily and rose
of "Lancelot and Elaine," and forward to the rank garden of
Ettarre. Through its suggestion of organic growth the image
undercuts the strangeness that Lancelot imputes to the
entwining of sin and purity and makes of their
interdependence something almost *natural*, "not to be
plucked asunder," an emblem of the human condition.
Lancelot strives to part them, and the striving is the essence
of his greatness, although in so doing he necessarily tears
himself asunder. For in the moral world of the *Idylls* purity

and sin, like greatness and guilt, truth and untruth, honor and dishonor, are no longer polar opposites. Only Galahad and Modred preserve the absoluteness of the distinctions, but they are very loosely linked to the Round Table, Galahad ascending to the spiritual city and Modred ever waiting to inherit the infernal city which is rightfully his.

Tennyson never attempts to portray Lancelot after he attains to the holiness of Galahad, reputed by some to be his son (HG, 144). Lancelot's transformation, unlike Guinevere's, takes place offstage, but it is implicit in all that follows "The Holy Grail": his sparing of Pelleas, the confrontation with Tristram in "The Last Tournament," and his final parting from the Queen in "Guinevere." Again the initiative belongs to Guinevere, who flees to the convent at Almesbury while he, "love-loyal to [her] least wish" (125), returns to his estates.

The problem which Tennyson prudently avoids with Lancelot he confronts head-on with Guinevere, whose conversion takes place before our eyes. In part Tennyson is the victim of his own success. To the extent that Guinevere's regal dignity and unabashed sensuality convince us, we resent her groveling in contrition at Arthur's feet. Arthur presents the same problem in reverse. He has until now been largely recessed from our sight, acting less as a character within the poem than as a semidivine presence hovering over it, shaping it, the point of ideal reference by which we measure the men and women in it. But in "Guinevere" the "great Sun of Glory" (GL, 22) is compelled to play the role of injured husband; symbol and character, demigod and cuckold clash, and for an excruciating instant we catch a glimpse of Christ with horns.

An inevitable duality in Arthur's character runs throughout the *Idylls.* Tennyson himself was aware of the dilemma; according to his son Hallam, he thought he had perhaps failed to make clear "the real humanity of the King" and inserted in the Epilogue, as the last of his thousands of

revisions, the line "Ideal manhood closed in real man."[25]
Yet when, as in "Guinevere," Arthur must act as a "real
man," his divinity threatens to vanish before our eyes.
Conversely, when we become excessively conscious of his
ideality, his human anguish as wronged husband and
betrayed king fails to move us. To fulfill his function, Arthur
must be equally persuasive in his dual role of "highest and
most human too" (G, 644). In the frame poems Tennyson
risks obscuring Arthur's humanity by enveloping him in the
aura of divinity. In "Guinevere" he takes the opposite risk
of obscuring Arthur's divinity by stressing his troubled
humanity. The risk is inescapable, indeed inseparable from
the very conception of the King; at any moment in the poem
he is in double jeopardy of becoming either too "real" or
too remote.

Tennyson's aesthetic dilemma in properly distancing
Arthur is a direct consequence of patterning him upon the
paradoxical nature of Christ, the stern Judge and forgiving
Son. In the first part of his speech to Guinevere the King
figures as Christ in Judgment, in the second part, as Christ
in Mercy; in both parts the voice of Arthur the man can be
heard alongside that of the Christ-figure, first in injured
rage, then in compassion. The ferocity of Arthur's initial
denunciation of Guinevere is deliberately chilling, coming as
it does immediately after her anguished dialogue with the
novice has quickened our sympathy.[26] Yet her conscience
and her will are still deeply at odds, and it requires the final
onslaught of Arthur's words in the convent to precipitate her
salvation. She has sworn to suppress all thought of Lancelot
and "never to see him more, / To see him more" (374–375);
but her resolve, at first glance so emphatic in its
repetition, is in fact ambiguous. Even as she makes it,
Lancelot comes flooding into her memory in the richest of all
her recollections of their first meeting. Her reverie drifts
to her first sight of Arthur—

> . . . cold,
> High, self-contained, and passionless, not like him,
> "Not like my Lancelot"—
>
> (402–404)

at the very moment when the King's armor rings through the
corridors and he bears down upon her like an avenging
angel. Before this ominous apparition the Queen "grovelled
with her face against the floor" (412); the line is intentionally
shocking. The stately Queen writhes in bestial abasement,
as a few lines later she "creeps" closer and lays her hands
around Arthur's feet. Vivien had seduced Merlin in the
identical posture in which Guinevere now craves forgiveness
of Arthur, and Tennyson intends us to feel the same terrified
awe in the face of both scenes. In the first, the serpent-
temptress reenacts the Fall; in the second, the King in
Judgment bestrides Vice in the form of the fallen Guinevere.

From this stance Arthur speaks his cruelest lines, his
"hard sayings," as it were:

> "The children born of thee are sword and fire,
> Red ruin, and the breaking up of laws,
> The craft of kindred and the Godless hosts
> Of heathen swarming o'er the Northern Sea."
>
> (422–425)

However harsh Arthur's words, they come from a ghostly
voice out of the darkness that we know to be the King's and
that carries an authority even beyond the King's. The
problem, it seems to me, lies not in Arthur's fierceness but in
his forgiveness. His uneasy transition from King in
Judgment to King in Mercy is clearly marked by the blowing
of the distant trumpet in the pause between the two parts
of his speech. When Arthur goes on to say, "Lo! I forgive
thee, as Eternal God / Forgives" (541–542), he makes a
simile of that for which there can be no similitude, and he
leaves us as breathless as the man who boasts of his own
humility.[27] In "The Passing" we never question his right as

dying King to appropriate the words of the dying Christ—
"My God, thou hast forgotten me in my death" (27)—but as
cuckolded husband he cannot speak like a surrogate god.
It is worse still when he tries to speak like a "real man":

> O golden hair, with which I used to play
> Not knowing! O imperial-moulded form . . .
>
> (G, 544–545)

Tennyson wants us to believe that Arthur feels sexual passion
for Guinevere, and hence that both his injury and his
forgiveness are all the greater. But if we must take Arthur
on these terms, then he had no business losing Guinevere
in the first place, and he must stand judged by his wife's own
words: "cold . . . passionless . . . not like my Lancelot."

The heart of Arthur's denunciation of Guinevere is that
her adultery and its foul example have "spoilt the purpose of
my life" (450). Yet we cannot uncritically accept Arthur's
judgment in his own case, even though he is obviously
closer to the truth than is Vivien's counter-judgment:
"Man! is he man at all, who knows and winks?" (MV, 779).*

---

* Vivien's question slyly answers itself: she *asserts* that Arthur
knows and hence is cuckold, "coward, and fool" (MV, 787). But the
evidence is far from clear, and our judgment necessarily hinges
on two further questions: when the adultery first occurred and when
Arthur became aware of it. After his marriage, but as early in the
reign as "The Marriage of Geraint," a "rumour rose about the
Queen, / Touching her guilty love for Lancelot, / *Though yet there
lived no proof*" (24–26, italics added). Of the love between them
there is no doubt, but its consummation remains uncertain, although
distinctly possible, when Balin sees them in Guinevere's garden.
Yet the garden scene, however compromising, is not conclusive, for
we are told that Vivien "lied with ease" (BB, 517) in describing the
lovers' embraces to Balin. The same uncertain shadow of guilt hangs
over the scene in which Vivien asks Merlin if he has heard the
whispers of Lancelot's "commerce with the Queen" (MV, 768).
Merlin's equivocal reply—"let them be" (775)—heightens the probability
of the adultery, but Vivien is a slanderer and Merlin's weakened will
doubtless cripples his resistance to her charges. By the time of
"Lancelot and Elaine" the Queen and Lancelot are clearly lovers,

Judged by his own high standards, the "blameless King" (MV, 777) is more than once at fault, although his faults are the defects of his virtues, as when he wholly misapprehends Vivien's intentions. Both Vivien and Dagonet call him a fool; they are both right and wrong, and they both mean very different things by the term.

We have only to consider the catastrophic miscarriage of Arthur's designs to realize how heavily Tennyson has hedged his King in ambiguity. The causes of the catastrophe are multiple, and Arthur is never more blind to this complexity than when he concludes his denunciation of Guinevere, "And all through thee!"* (490). Under the particular circumstances the charge is cruel; under any circumstances it is simplistic. The very profusion and variety of evil throughout the

---

and although Arthur has grounds to suspect them, he remains unaware of the connection.

Indisputable evidence of the adultery comes very much later than we at first realize. For although "Lancelot and Elaine" occurs in the middle of the sequence of the idylls, the events within it take place near the end (the tenth year) of Arthur's reign. Lancelot is absent on the Grail quest in the following year, after which Arthur leads the expedition against Pelleas. Once Arthur learns of the adultery at the end of "The Last Tournament," he acts with dispatch, riding off to Almesbury and denouncing Guinevere. Vivien's "winking" King is clearly a slander, although it might be urged that the reader ought not to have to make the discovery in a footnote such as this. Conversely, he ought not to need warning against Vivien as a witness. The essential point is that Tennyson so finely balances the evidence that each reader judges Arthur according to his lights, although only the dimmest of us could mistake him for a *mari complaisant*. Despite the complexity of the presentation we have little difficulty in choosing between two errors in judgment that Tennyson invites us to connect: Vivien's base assumption that Balin has slept with the Queen and Arthur's too trusting assumption that his noblest knight has not.

* Throughout the speech Arthur sounds a little like Milton's God absolving Himself of all responsibility for the Fall. Both poets falter at this point for similar reasons, but Milton has the advantage of putting his bad arguments in God's mouth while Tennyson must put his in Arthur's.

Idylls—one thinks of the sinister, innumerable Powers of the North—belie Arthur's charge. The ultimate flaw in the kingdom lies not only in Guinevere but in the human seed that also breeds Mark and Modred, and in the mortality that erodes even as it gives preciousness to human aspiration.

While Mark and Modred have reason to hate Arthur, the strength of their malice far exceeds the adequacy of their motives. Here one begins to appreciate Tennyson's wisdom in not following Malory in making Arthur the incestuous father of Modred. As Tennyson saw it, Arthur is destroyed not for his wickedness but for the vulnerability of his virtues, and hence the incest is fundamentally irrelevant to his fate. Swinburne brilliantly but sophistically argues the opposite view, claiming that the "hinge of the whole legend" is Modred's incestuous birth and that "from the sin of Arthur's youth proceeds the ruin of his reign and realm." [28] But this reduces tragedy to a kind of moralistic bookkeeping, whereas its essence is not that the punishment should fit the crime but that it vastly and inexplicably exceeds it. Arthur's "crime" is his noble delusion that he can remake the fallen, intractable world, and it is this world, symbolized by Modred, that finally rises up to destroy him.

With the trumpet-summons to the Last Battle, Arthur rides from the convent and Guinevere sees his outline vanish in the mist, but not "the face, / Which then was as an angel's" (592).* Successively divested of wife, home, companions, city, and kingdom, the transfigured Arthur moves once again through that ghostly medium in which he has always appeared most substantial. The parting from Guinevere is the necessary prelude to his disincarnation, just as the marriage served as his incarnation, a kind of self-engendered second birth complete with pangs:

---

* Just before St. Stephen is martyred, "all that sat in the council, looking steadfastly on him, saw his face as it had been the face of an angel" (Acts 6:15).

> And Arthur, passing thence to battle, felt
> Travail, and throes and agonies of the life,
> Desiring to be joined with Guinevere.
>
> (CA, 74–76)

The marriage has the same strange impersonality as the parting at Almesbury; Arthur chooses his Queen much as Zeus chose Leda, taking her less as wife than as medium through which Spirit might wed Flesh and work its will in the mortal world. With the end of the marriage, he is again "vext with waste dreams" (CA, 84), as he was in "The Coming." The dreams, however, are not of his ruined marriage but of his shattered kingdom. He can survive Guinevere but not the loss of "the goodliest fellowship of famous knights / Whereof this world holds record" (PA, 183–184). The destruction of the Round Table inspires his most poignant lines, and in this Tennyson remains strikingly true to Malory, whose Arthur is "sorrier for my good knights' loss than for the loss of my fair queen; for queens I might have enow, but such a fellowship of good knights shall never be together in no company."[29]

VI · *Symbol and Story*

In the most prominent position in the *Idylls*—the first
word of the first line—Tennyson places a minor character
who never again appears after "The Coming of Arthur." Yet
if Leodogran quickly passes from the poem, his dream does
not. Narratively he has no function other than consenting
to his daughter's marriage to the King. Symbolically, he
remains ever-present, for as he nods and drowses, his dream
prefigures the entire poem. The seeming insignificance of
Leodogran illustrates with striking clarity three principles
which constitute the underlying structure of the *Idylls*. No
character ever appears only once but instead recurs in the
guise of another character or through the reappearance of an
image or event with which he is associated. No action occurs
uniquely but instead reverberates, in anticipation or
retrospect, throughout the poem. No symbol stands for one
thing only without also containing its opposite. The deeper
one penetrates the *Idylls*, the more one perceives that
its interrelations are inexhaustible, that each of its parts
reflects the infinite complexity of the whole.

In the chaos preceding Arthur's reign, Leodogran is all but
annihilated by a heathen horde that, "reddening the sun
with smoke and earth with blood" (CA, 37), bears down
upon his kingdom. Leodogran incorporates this "actual"
landscape of blood and fire into his dream, in which "a

phantom king" (CA, 429) is enveloped in the flames of war. Down to the minutest phrase the dream foretells events to come, including the final event in which the King looms like "the phantom of a Giant" (G, 598) in the mists of the Last Battle. Between Leodogran's prophetic sleep and the Last Battle, his dream takes root in the mind of Pelleas, who dreams of Arthur's hall bursting into flames (PE, 507), and is then reborn in Leodogran's daughter Guinevere, who in a nightmare sees her own shadow engulfing whole cities in fire (G, 80–82). First generated by an actual event in the narrative (the flames of civil war in which Leodogran is attacked by his brother Urien), the dream invades the consciousness of other characters and then reenters the action of the poem as brother slays brother in "Balin and Balan" and Lancelot wages civil war against his King.

The structure of the *Idylls* everywhere mirrors its meaning. Hence in his poem in which shadow and substance continually reverse their meaning, dreams and actions are indistinguishable because ultimately identical. Whether Leodogran dreams the *Idylls of the King* or his dream is an event within it depends entirely upon one's point of view. Throughout the poem dreams and symbols become literalized in events, which in turn generate the dreams and symbols that are enmeshed in the narrative. Tristram's dream in "The Last Tournament" illustrates this principle in a single idyll, just as Leodogran's dream illustrates it in the larger compass of the entire poem. Asleep in the woodland lodge in which he had formerly made love to Isolt, Tristram dreams of presenting her with a ruby necklace, which turns to frozen blood in her hands (412). As Tristram sleeps, the action shifts to the opposite end of the kingdom, where Arthur attacks the Red Knight of the North. But Tristram's dream of blood and guilt continues to color this parallel strand of the narrative, in which Arthur's "blood-red" adversary (442) is slaughtered and his hall rings with the shrieks of his massacred followers. The action then returns

to Tristram, but with so deft an interweaving of the two
narrative strands that it is as if the dreaming Tristram were
awakened by distant shouts from the Red Knight's hall:

> Then, out of Tristram waking, the red dream
> Fled with a shout, and that low lodge returned,
> Mid-forest, and the wind among the boughs.
>
> (486–488)

Two events widely spaced geographically but temporally
simultaneous—Tristram's journey westward to Tintagil and
Arthur's to the North—are fused in Tristram's dream, which
in turn propels the narrative into the future, as Tristram
rides from the forest to his impending slaughter at the hands
of the shrieking Mark.

A similar fusion of dream and action occurs in the garden
scene in "Balin and Balan." Chilled by Lancelot's hesitancy
in approaching her, Guinevere rebukes his aloofness with
a simile: "ye stand, fair lord, as in a dream" (253). The
phrase is at once figurative and literal, for Guinevere's words
and the lilies by which Lancelot pauses have reawakened
his dream of the previous night, when he saw the Virgin
standing "with lily in hand" (255–256). The transition
between dream and waking life in the garden continues in
"Lancelot and Elaine," where Lancelot's dream of the Virgin
materializes in the narrative in the form of the virginal
Elaine, who with lily in hand floats past him in death.
Finally, the dream is commemorated in an imaginary art that
extends beyond the art of the poem itself as Arthur directs
that the lily of Elaine be sculpted on her tomb.

As dreams have the power of actualizing themselves in
the narrative, so symbols take on a life of their own,
momentarily usurping the role of the person or thing they
symbolize. Throughout the *Idylls* the worm or serpent
bears its traditional significance, and worms within gardens
are emblematic of the Fall.[1] But the peculiarly Tennysonian
use of the symbol occurs in the last of the garden scenes,

in which Modred is half-metamorphosed back into the serpent that he symbolizes. Clothed in green, he "couches" high on the wall of Guinevere's garden, where Lancelot discovers him and, plucking the symbol from the wall, "cast[s] him as a worm upon the way" (G, 35).

The inner temper of the characters continually manifests itself in the outward action of the poem. Lancelot, for example, enters the Tournament of Diamonds as a kind of moral cripple; his spiritual wound becomes palpably physical as his own "kith and kin" (LE, 464), emblematic of his divided, guilt-ridden self, bear down upon him and leave him all but dead upon the field. Lancelot's self-struggle intensifies in "The Holy Grail," where, on the steps of the Grail castle, he is confronted by two great lions that rise "upright like a man" (818) and threaten to tear him to pieces. It is as if the rampant lions emblazoned on his shield have come to furious life. The man and his animate emblem grapple with one another much as Balin struggles to suppress, but finally becomes, the savage heraldic beast painted on his shield.

From the synoptic perspective in which we are now viewing the *Idylls*, character cannot be abstracted from symbol and both have no substance apart from the narrative in which they are embedded. In essence the narrative is a sequence of symbols protracted in time, the symbolism a kind of condensed narration. The story functions like the melody in a game of musical chairs, with the dramatis personae exchanging roles as they move from one position to the next. However outlandish, this image figures in the poem itself as the vacant chair, carved with curious figures, which Merlin made and named "The Siege perilous"; he sits in it and is lost forever, Galahad sits and is saved (HG, 168–178). The story of the novice knight and the scornful lady provides a similar narrative matrix; the young Gareth is formed within it and emerges unscathed, whereas the fledgling Pelleas is destroyed in the identical role.

The narrative generates a limited number of these themes, with the characters providing the variations. The result is a balance of novelty and continuity in which seemingly new characters enter seemingly new situations while the reader subliminally experiences the pleasures of recurrence. Frequently one character will pick up phrases or whole lines previously spoken by another, but the context totally reverses their significance. Just before Galahad ascends to "the spiritual city," he echoes Jesus' words—"my time is hard at hand"—a line which Modred repeats verbatim as he plots to destroy the kingdom.[2] Feigning love for Merlin but in fact seeking to undo him, Vivien bids him a pretended farewell and says, "My fate or folly . . . / . . . must be to love thee still" (MV, 925–926); still loving Guinevere and striving to save her, Arthur confesses on parting, "My doom is, I love thee still" (G, 556). Parallelism of gesture reinforces the verbal parallelisms in these contrapuntal scenes of seduction and salvation. Both farewells culminate in the casting of a spell, Vivien's over Merlin and Arthur's over Guinevere. After Merlin yields, Vivien

> put forth the charm
> Of woven paces and of waving hands,
> And in the hollow oak he lay as dead.
>
> (MV, 965–967)

As Guinevere grovels at Arthur's feet, recalling the posture of Vivien entwined about Merlin's,[3] she feels the King's breath upon her neck,

> And in the darkness o'er her fallen head,
> Perceived the waving of his hands that blest.
>
> (G, 579–580)

The apparent profusion of individual characters in the *Idylls* is sheer Tennysonian sleight of hand. For the same characters recur, transformed into their opposites, or undergo metamorphoses before our eyes only to emerge in new guises, like Gareth, who first plays the part of a kitchen-knave, reveals himself to be the noble nephew of Arthur, is recast as Pelleas, and finally appears as the Red Knight, the antitype of Arthur. In the last analysis, there are no individual characters in the *Idylls*, only juxtaposed relationships in which diametrically opposite characters often share the same symbolism. Arthur is the Sun-King but his adversary Vivien is a sun-worshipper who praises the fire of heaven and wears a clasp of gold—one of Arthur's emblems —in her hair (MV, 219). "The Bright one in the highest," as Tennyson wrote in "Demeter and Persephone," "Is brother of the Dark one in the lowest."

The archetype of all relationships in the *Idylls* is the triangle of Arthur-Guinevere-Lancelot, of which the many other triangles are variants. Extending beyond this primal triangle, each of the principals gives rise to secondary characters who are their analogues or antitypes. Thus Arthur is reduplicated in his nephew, Gareth, and, by antithesis, in Gareth's brother, Modred. The mixed potentialities of Guinevere's nature reappear in the false Ettarre and the faithful Enid. Finally, Arthur and Lancelot set the pattern for all fraternal relationships that become fratricidal, as embodied microcosmically in Balin and Balan and macrocosmically in the civil wars that destroy the Round Table.

The central triangle is mirrored most clearly in "The Last Tournament," where the two sets of kings, queens, and false knights play out their parts in alternate paragraphs of the narrative. Lancelot sits on the absent Arthur's throne as he presides over the tournament in which Tristram is the victor, and in Tristram's ironic address to Lancelot— "Great brother . . . / Be happy in thy fair Queen as I in mine" (203–204)—the two triangles are neatly joined.[4] "The Last Tournament" in turn recapitulates the setting in "Lancelot and Elaine," where Arthur presides over the

Tournament of Diamonds and the victorious Lancelot is torn between Guinevere and Elaine, precisely as Tristram hesitates between Isolt his wife and Isolt the queen of Mark.

All three triangles are linked to the love triangle in "Pelleas and Ettarre," and hence also to its companion idyll, "Gareth and Lynette." Both Gareth and Pelleas pattern themselves on Arthur; the confident Gareth imitates the young King in his triumphant battles, and the shattered Pelleas, a "moral child" betrayed by Ettarre, a debased version of Guinevere, parallels Arthur's later decline. Even before he encounters Ettarre in the torrid forest, Pelleas foretells his fate in lines that clearly link him to Arthur: "O my Queen, my Guinevere, / For I will be thine Arthur when we meet" (PE, 44–45). The link is tightened by the identical roles played by the false friend in both triangles: Pelleas sends Gawain as his emissary to Ettarre, precisely as Arthur, with the same fatal result, sent Lancelot to Guinevere.*

Before marshaling his forces for the Last Battle, Arthur

---

* If Arthur is the exemplar of both Gareth and Pelleas, Guinevere is the type of Lynette and Ettarre in her incapacity to see beyond outward appearance. Because Arthur passes before her without the emblems of his royalty, "She saw him not, or marked not, if she saw" (CA, 53). So, too, Lynette initially scorns the noble Gareth, mistaking him for the kitchen-knave he pretends to be, and, like Guinevere, desires instead the service of Lancelot.

Lancelot supplies the common bond in this series of interconnected narratives. At the apex of the triangle in "Lancelot and Elaine," he also provides the point where the double triangles join in "The Last Tournament." He befriends Gareth, lending him his shield and charger, forming a counterpoint to Gawain, who borrows Pelleas' horse and armor only to betray him. Finally, Lancelot unhorses both Gareth and Pelleas in their respective idylls, but whereas Gareth rejoices that he has been overthrown by so noble a knight, Pelleas shrieks in rage over falling before so adulterous a traitor. For an admirable account of such parallel patterns of narrative and characterization, see Kenneth Alan Robb, "The Structure of Tennyson's *Idylls of the King*" (Ph.D. diss., University of Wisconsin, 1966), *passim*. Robb refers to such patterns as "correspondences," and a cluster of these correspondences he calls a "narrative image" (p. 32).

remarks to Bedivere, "The king who fights his people fights himself" (PA, 72). He has just come from waging bitter war with Lancelot, a struggle that both recognize as suicidal. The kingdom had been founded upon the strength of their vows and those of Arthur and Guinevere. King and chief knight, and King and Queen, pledge "deathless love" in phrases that are virtually identical (CA, 131, 467–469). At one point Arthur addresses Lancelot with an intimacy of affection that borders on the language of romantic love: "Lancelot, my Lancelot, thou in whom I have / Most joy and most affiance" (LE, 1345–1346). Each has saved the other's life in battle, and Lancelot is Arthur's "noblest brother," his "right arm" (GL, 553; G, 426). Injury to the one is, inevitably, injury to the other, and only in Lancelot's absence could Modred have struck the blow that fells the King.

Struggling to break his ties to Guinevere, Lancelot at the end of "Lancelot and Elaine" prays that God

> send a sudden Angel down
> To seize me by the hair and bear me far,
> And fling me deep in that forgotten mere,
> Among the tumbled fragments of the hills.
>
> (1413–1416)

The lines are strikingly premonitory of the landscape of the poem's close. Surrounded by tumbled fragments of hills, the Lady of the Lake, Lancelot's foster-mother, rises from the mere and, as if in answer to his prayer, receives Arthur's "right arm"—Excalibur. Only Bedivere, the first-created of the knights, survives to witness Arthur's passing. A minor figure who appears exclusively in "The Coming" and "The Passing," Bedivere is the embodiment of fidelity, an adjunct to the King and the antitype of the absent Lancelot. But fidelity is the most ephemeral of virtues in the *Idylls* and hence Arthur, after the shock of Lancelot's betrayal, wrongly accuses Bedivere of treachery, the last and most poignant of Arthur's errors.

To Bedivere is left the burden of perpetuating the King's story. The nominal narrator of "The Passing," Bedivere has already moved in time beyond the world of the *Idylls*, in which he figures as both actor and chronicler.[5] In the "white winter" of old age, he recounts the history of the King to alien peoples with "new faces, other minds" (PA, 5). As the poem closes, the legend of Arthur becomes self-perpetuating and cannot be confined to any single source, be it Bedivere, the omniscient narrator, or that nameless bard—"he that tells the tale"[6]—to whom Tennyson repeatedly refers and who is at once Malory, Tennyson himself, and the great chain of Arthurian chroniclers and poets who preceded him.

The *Idylls* not only retells Arthurian legend but recreates the process by which myths are made. One sees this process at work in the many scenes that recall the former splendor of the Round Table even as it vanishes in flames. Thus Arthur, alone with Guinevere at Almesbury, denounces her for destroying the glorious company that once had "serve[d] as model for the mighty world" (G, 462); when Arthur is later placed in the funeral barge, Bedivere, as if he had overheard Arthur at Almesbury, incorporates the line in his lament for the dying King (PA, 403), for the words are now a canonical part of Arthur's legend, transmitted whole from character to character and place to place. As the realm moves ever closer to extinction, the characters themselves become increasingly concerned with the perpetuation of Arthur's story—and hence of Tennyson's poem. Bedivere fears to discard Excalibur lest all relics of the King be lost and only "empty breath / And rumours of a doubt" survive his passing (PA, 267–268). After ordering Bedivere to fling the sword into the mere, Arthur remarks, as if shaping the legend of which he is himself the subject,

> And, wheresoever I am sung or told
> In aftertime, this also shall be known.[7]
>
> (PA, 202–203)

Characters within the larger fiction of the *Idylls* often
generate lesser fictions within it, like mirrors within mirrors.
At the start of Percivale's narrative of the Grail quest, the
skeptical Ambrosius points out that the ancient monastic
records seem "mute of this miracle" (HG, 66). Ambrosius
functions as a foil to Percivale's sister, the holy nun whose
vision not only transmits but in part creates the legend of the
Grail. The strength of her own belief, communicated through
the spell she casts over Galahad, leads directly to the quest.
An enchantress, she is the Merlin of the Grail, summoning
the quest into being through her myth-making powers,
exactly as Merlin creates Camelot and Tennyson the
entire poem.

At the heart of Arthur's story is the dual cycle of his
coming and promised return. The *Idylls*, incorporating this
cycle into its structure, is itself a kind of literary second
coming of Arthur, a resurrection in Victorian England of the
long sequence of Arthuriads extending back before Malory
and forward through Spenser, Dryden, Scott, and Tennyson.
The poem takes on the quality of a self-fulfilling prophecy
and validates itself, like Scripture, by foretelling in one
passage what is fulfilled in the next. Dreams most clearly
serve this prophetic function, but the various songs
interspersed throughout the *Idylls* also anticipate and
symbolize the action. Although formally set off from the
narrative by rhyme, the songs are in fact lyric condensations
of the idylls in which they appear, like "A Worm within
the Rose," which foreshadows Pelleas' discovery of Gawain
sleeping with Ettarre among the roses.[8]

This capacity of the *Idylls* to symbolize itself is everywhere
apparent. The allegorical figure of Time carved in the
hermit's cave (GL, 1166–1170) casts in relief the theme of
"Gareth and Lynette" and of the entire poem; so, too, the
twelve great windows commemorating Arthur's battles
mirror the twelve-fold division of the *Idylls* and lend a kind
of fictive historicity to the King's victories (HG, 248–250).

Like the sculptured effigy of Elaine, works of art within the poem memorialize the work of art that *is* the poem. A final image emblematic of the whole occurs in the very center of the *Idylls,* in Vivien's love song to Merlin. Vivien interrupts her song to remark that it resembles a fair necklace of the Queen's

> That burst in dancing, and the pearls were spilt;
> Some lost, some stolen, some as relics kept.
> . . . so it is with this rhyme:
> It lives dispersedly in many hands,
> And every minstrel sings it differently.
>   (MV, 450–451, 453–455)

The fair necklace symbolizes the quintessential matter of Arthurian legend. Deformed by time, retold in fragments by countless minstrels, the myth was at length shaped by Tennyson into the perfect circle of the *Idylls.*

Notes

Bibliography

Index

Notes

I · Dispelling the Mists

1. F. R. Leavis, *New Bearings in English Poetry*, 2nd ed. (London, Chatto & Windus, 1950), p. 175.

2. *The Letters of W. B. Yeats,* ed. Allan Wade (New York, Macmillan, 1955), p. 218. When Yeats was asked late in life whom he had venerated as a young man, the answer "came without hesitation, 'Tennyson.' On the question being repeated by the enquirer, who had not expected this answer, the reply was the same with the addition of 'Wordsworth.'" Joseph Hone, *W. B. Yeats* (London, Macmillan, 1942), p. 34.

3. Leavis, *New Bearings*, pp. 25–26.

4. T. S. Eliot, "In Memoriam," *Selected Essays*, 3rd. ed. (London, Faber and Faber, 1951), p. 337.

5. For additional echoes of Tennyson in Eliot's verse, see Benjamin DeMott, "The Voice of Lotos-Land," *Hells and Benefits* (New York, Basic Books, 1958), pp. 247–264, and W. K. Wimsatt's admirable "*Prufrock* and *Maud:* From Plot to Symbol," *Hateful Contraries* (Lexington, Ky., University of Kentucky Press, 1965), pp. 201–212. The influence of *Maud* on "Prufrock" seems undeniable both in overall design and in verbal detail. The famous description in "Prufrock" beginning, "The yellow fog that rubs its back upon the window-panes," finds its likely source in *Maud,* pt. II, sec. iv, st. 9: "And the yellow vapours choke / The great city sounding wide." Even in his most Eliotic moments of ironic self-mockery, Prufrock sounds uncannily like the narrator in *Maud:*

Should I fear to greet my friend
Or to say, 'Forgive the wrong'? . . .

And I loathe the squares and streets,
And the faces that one meets . . .
(Maud, pt. II, sec. iv, st. 12–13)

There will be time, there will be time
To prepare a face to meet the faces that you meet . . .

Should I, after tea and cakes and ices,
Have the strength to force the moment to its crisis?
("Prufrock")

Eliot's indebtedness to *Maud* is also evident in *The Waste Land*. For example, "Mix not memory with doubt" in *Maud* (pt. II, sec. iv, st. 8) becomes, at the start of *The Waste Land*, "mixing / Memory and desire." One of Eliot's "Notes on *The Waste Land*" suggests that he was indebted to Tennyson for far more than occasional phrasing. Eliot explains that "Tiresias, although a mere spectator and not indeed a 'character,' is yet the most important personage in the poem," combining in himself all the other characters. This structural innovation—Eliot's daring breakdown of conventional narrative in order to convey the disjunctive rhythms of consciousness itself—undoubtedly owes much to *Maud*. Tennyson subtitled the poem "A Monodrama" and explained that its uniqueness lay in the fact "that different phases of passion in one person take the place of different characters" (Christopher Ricks, ed., *The Poems of Tennyson* [London, Longmans, 1969], p. 1039). Apart from Tennyson's own description, the most apt characterization of *Maud* is, ironically, Leavis' of *The Waste Land:* "The unity the poet aims at is that of an inclusive consciousness: the organization it achieves as a work of art is . . . musical" (*New Bearings*, p. 103). The originality of *Maud*, however, has been obscured by its incongruously conventional plot, which is pure melodrama. Within a few months of finishing *Maud*, Tennyson began work on the *Idylls of the King*, in which he perfected the techniques of split characterization and multiple consciousness that Eliot was to employ in "Prufrock" and *The Waste Land*.

6. Eliot, *Selected Essays*, pp. 337, 331.

7. Ibid., pp. 337–338.

8. Hallam Tennyson, *Alfred, Lord Tennyson: A Memoir*, 2 vols. (London, Macmillan, 1898), II, 132.
9. Harold Nicolson, *Tennyson: Aspects of His Life, Character and Poetry* (London, Constable and Constable, 1923), pp. 231–232.
10. H. Tennyson, *Memoir*, II, 128.
11. Nicolson, *Tennyson: Aspects*, pp. 27–29.
12. Eliot, *Selected Essays*, p. 336.
13. Cited in Ricks, *Poems*, pp. 859–860.
14. Cited in Graham Hough, "Introduction," *George Meredith: Selected Poems* (London, Oxford University Press, 1962), p. 11. The sharp division of opinion the *Idylls* has aroused since its first publication reflects something of the teasing ambiguity of the poem. There are those who, like Thackeray, moved by delight and two bottles of claret, praised Tennyson for his "heroes and beauties and purple landscapes . . . Every step I have walked in Elfland has been a sort of Paradise to me." (H. Tennyson, *Memoir*, I, 445.) In opposite reaction to the same surface polish of the *Idylls*, Carlyle deplored their "inward perfection of vacancy"; Tennyson had treated his reader like an infant, although "the lollipops were so superlative." (Joseph Slater, ed., *The Correspondence of Emerson and Carlyle* [New York, Columbia University Press, 1964], p. 553.) Something of the same impatience comes through Hopkins' celebrated remark that, although Tennyson will be recognized as "one of our greatest poets," he should have entitled the poem "*Charades from the Middle Ages*." (Claude C. Abbott, ed., *The Correspondence of Gerard Manley Hopkins and Richard Watson Dixon* [London, Oxford University Press, 1935], p. 24.) Swinburne managed to have it both ways by attacking the grotesque immorality of the *Idylls* ("every virtue is made to seem either imbecile or vile") while at the same time dismissing the poem as an innocuous "*Morte d'Albert, or Idylls of the Prince Consort*." ("Under the Microscope," *The Complete Works of Algernon Charles Swinburne*, Bonchurch Edition, vol. XVI, ed. Sir Edmund Gosse and Thomas James Wise [London, Heinemann, 1925–1926], p. 407, and John D. Jump, ed., *Tennyson: The Critical Heritage* [London, Routledge & Kegan Paul, 1967], p. 339.) For Whitman, the *Idylls* was Tennyson's finest work and its creator would "give illustriousness, through the long roll of time, to our Nineteenth Century." (Jump, *Tennyson*, p. 350.) Henry James's faint praise of the style and craftsmanship of the *Idylls*—"If one surrenders one's sense to their perfect picturesqueness, it is the most charming poetry in the

world" (Jerome H. Buckley, *Tennyson: The Growth of a Poet* [Cambridge, Mass., Harvard University Press, 1960], p. 191)—contrasts with Gladstone's high praise of the poem's depths: "Its author, by his own single strength, has made a sensible addition to the permanent wealth of mankind" (Jump, *Tennyson*, p. 266). Cf. Jowett's comment that "Tennyson has made the Arthur legend a great revelation of human experience." (Paull F. Baum, *Tennyson: Sixty Years After* [Chapel Hill, N.C., University of North Carolina Press, 1948], p. 202).

15. H. Tennyson, *Memoir*, I, 453–454.

16. The same unevenness of quality separates the original version of "The Passing of Arthur," published in 1842 as the "Morte d'Arthur," from "The Epic," which introduces it. "The Epic" is a brief, curiously embarrassed and embarrassing domestic idyll set "at Francis Allen's on the Christmas-eve," where one of Allen's guests, who is clearly Tennyson himself, is persuaded to read part of his epic on King Arthur, which he then does in the "Morte." The décor of "The Epic" is entirely modern, which is to say Victorian-contemporary, and the poem has the same self-conscious modernity as the other "English Idyls" with which it was published. But the instant "The Epic" ends and the "Morte d'Arthur" abruptly begins—"So all day long the noise of battle rolled"—we enter a world immeasurably more remote in time than the world of "The Epic," yet immeasurably closer to our own. In 1842 Tennyson lacked the courage to be unequivocally "escapist," and hence the Victorian realism of "The Epic" is quaintly dated, whereas the Arthurian archaism of the "Morte" has the continuing relevance of all great literature.

II · Evolving the Form

1. H. Tennyson, *Memoir*, I, 453n.

2. Ibid., II, 128.

3. Kathleen Tillotson, "Tennyson's Serial Poem," *Mid-Victorian Studies* (London, University of London, Athlone Press, 1965), p. 109.

4. See ibid., pp. 86–88.

5. Hallam Tennyson's gloss on the stanza, which he gives as the poet "gave it to me," lifts this interpretation out of the realm of speculation: "Here my father united the two Arthurs, the Arthur of the Idylls and the Arthur 'the man he held as half divine.'" (H. Tennyson, *Memoir*, I, xiv–xv.) Fifty years before

writing in "Merlin and the Gleam" of the adored friend who "cannot die," Tennyson had used exactly the same phrase to describe the mythical king in the "Morte d'Arthur." The poet has a dream-vision in which the king returns "thrice as fair" from Avilion and is greeted with the words, "Arthur is come again: he cannot die." Still another variant (unpublished) of this line— ". . . *our* Arthur cannot die" (italics added)—appears in the Trinity College Library, Tennyson MS. 0.15.39.

6. Composed when Tennyson was between fifteen and seventeen and published in *Poems by Two Brothers* (1827). Dating from the same period, the recently published "Napoleon's Retreat from Moscow" belongs with this series. Cf. the lines which describe the deserted city as "wan / And pale and tenantless and void of Man." (Christopher Ricks, "The Tennyson Manuscripts," *Times Literary Supplement*, August 21, 1969, 919.)

7. Trinity College Library, unpublished Tennyson MS. 0.15.18. Quoted by permission of the Master and Fellows of Trinity College, Cambridge. Cf. the identical simile in *The Princess:* "There rose a shriek as of a city sacked" (sec. IV, 147). Although the prohibition on publication of the Trinity manuscripts has recently been lifted, the full text of "Armageddon" has yet to be published. The most sustained passage in the poem anticipatory of "The Passing of Arthur" describes "the annihilating anarchy" of war,

> . . . a thick day,
> Palled with dun wreaths of dusky fight, a day
> Of many thunders and confusèd noise,
> Of bloody grapplings in the interval
> Of the opposèd Battle . . .
>
> (sec. III, 14–18)

8. See the closing lines of "Oenone"; Leodogran's dream in "The Coming of Arthur" (432–438); Pelleas' dream in "Pelleas and Ettarre" (504–509); Guinevere's dream of burning cities in "Guinevere" (75–82); the close of "The Kraken," in which the sea-monster

> . . . will lie
> Battening upon huge seaworms in his sleep,
> Until the latter fire shall heat the deep;
> Then once by man and angels to be seen,
> In roaring he shall rise and on the surface die.

Cf. Revelation 8:8–9: "And the second angel sounded, and as it were a great mountain burning with fire was cast into the sea: and the third part of the sea became blood; And the third part of the creatures which were in the sea, and had life, died."

9. Cf. Revelation 16:18–20: "And there were voices, and thunders, and lightnings: and there was a great earthquake, such as was not since men were upon the earth . . . And the cities of the nations fell . . . And every island fled away, and the mountains were not found." In *In Memoriam*, Hallam, the imagined witness to the holocaust in sec. CXXVII, "smilest, knowing all is well." The apparently pyromaniacal smile is intended to shock the reader into the realization that Hallam is no longer merely human and comprehends the earth's going up in flames as part of God's larger design. Hence he *smilest*, exactly as the Angel in "Armageddon" looks on the Apocalypse he describes with an "ineffable smile" (sec. II, 55).

10. Hallam Tennyson reprints the prose sketch in *Memoir*, II, 122–123, and dates it as "about 1833," but it seems probable that the fragment is somewhat earlier and predates the "Morte d'Arthur." The image of the hollow mountain may have been suggested by a passage in Malory in which Arthur "dreamed a wonderful dream . . . that him seemed he sat upon a chaflet in a chair, and the chair was fast to a wheel [of Fortune] . . . and the king thought there was under him, far from him, an hideous deep black water, and therein were all manner of serpents . . . foul and horrible; and suddenly the king thought the wheel turned up so down, and he fell among the serpents, and every beast took him by a limb." (Bk. XXI, ch. 3.)

11. The poem gained for Tennyson the Chancellor's Gold Medal at Cambridge in 1829. The prize cost him little effort since, in his own words, he won it by "the turning of an old poem on 'Armageddon' into 'Timbuctoo' by a little alteration of the beginning and the end." (H. Tennyson, *Memoir*, II, 355.)

12. H. Tennyson, *Memoir*, II, 125. Of Tennyson's three Arthurian poems roughly contemporary with the "Morte d'Arthur" —"The Lady of Shalott," "Sir Launcelot and Queen Guinevere," and "Sir Galahad"—only the first has any intrinsic interest, and it is far closer to Tennyson's private concerns as a poet than it is to Arthurian romance. "I met the story first in some Italian *novelle*," he told F. J. Furnival; "but the web, mirror, island, etc., were my own. Indeed, I doubt whether I should ever have put it in that shape if I had been then aware of the Maid of Astolat

in *Mort Arthur"* (Ricks, *Poems*, p. 354). It would be of interest to know precisely when the poem was begun (Ricks's "written by *c.* May 1832" slips out of one's hands) since that would establish a firm *earliest* date for Tennyson's reading of Malory, or at least of bk. XVIII, in which the lily-maid's story appears. Kathleen Tillotson (*Studies*, p. 85) suggests that all three poems belong to Tennyson's Cambridge period; at any rate, they quite evidently predate the "Morte d'Arthur."

13. Tennyson had additional motives for so diffidently introducing the "Morte." He was understandably cautious about introducing the reader to the then unfamiliar subject of Arthur. (Tillotson, *Studies*, p. 82.) He was also attempting, ineffectually as it turned out, to disarm his critics by anticipating their charge that he was escaping into the past:

> Why take the style of those heroic times?
> For nature brings not back the Mastodon,
> Nor we those times; and why should any man
> Remodel models?

14. H. Tennyson, *Memoir*, II, 89–90; W. J. Rolfe, ed., *The Poetic and Dramatic Works of Alfred, Lord Tennyson* (Boston and New York, Houghton Mifflin, 1898), p. 849. The most important of the reviews that stopped Tennyson was John Sterling's in the *Quarterly Review* of September 1842. But the review scarcely gave grounds for so drastic a result. "The miraculous legend of 'Excalibur,'" Sterling wrote, "does not come very near to us, and as reproduced by any modern writer must be a mere ingenious exercise of fancy. The poem, however, is full of distinct and striking description, perfectly expressed."

15. H. Tennyson, *Memoir*, II, 133; cf. I, 483.

16. Between 1833 and 1859 Tennyson was also deeply engaged in writing his elegy to the *other* Arthur, in substantially revising the *Poems* of 1832, composing new poems for the 1842 volume, and writing *The Princess* (1847) and *Maud, and Other Poems* (1855).

17. H. Tennyson, *Memoir*, II, 123–125.

18. Ibid., pp. 126–127. In a less familiar and stronger version of this passage, Tennyson complains that the commentators "have explained many things too allegorically." (H. Tennyson, *Materials for a Life of A. T.* [privately printed, 1895], II, 259.)

19. H. Tennyson, *Memoir*, II, 127.

20. Ricks, *Poems*, p. 1464.

21. Ryals, *From the Great Deep*, p. 121. I must in fairness add that this excerpt is not at all representative of the quality of insight elsewhere in the book.

22. Merriman, "The Faultless King: Tennyson and the Matter of Britain," unpub. ms., no pagination.

23. Ibid.

24. Henry Alford, in an article on the *Idylls* that Tennyson praised (*Contemporary Review*, 13 [1870], 107); F. E. L. Priestley, "Tennyson's *Idylls*," *Critical Essays on the Poetry of Tennyson*, ed. John Killham (London, Routledge & Kegan Paul, 1960), p. 242. Although I believe that Priestley errs in describing the *Idylls* as "primarily allegorical" (Killham, *Critical Essays*, p. 240), his essay remains most illuminating. The best case against reading the *Idylls* as allegory has been made by S. C. Burchell, "Tennyson's 'Allegory in the Distance,'" *PMLA*, 68 (1953), 418–424. Burchell takes his title from a letter of Jowett to Tennyson: "The allegory in the distance *greatly strengthens, also elevates, the meaning of the poem.*" (H. Tennyson, *Memoir*, I, 449.)

25. "Lancelot and Elaine" was published together with the Geraint idylls, "Merlin and Vivien," and "Guinevere." The reader, if he recalled the earlier "Morte d'Arthur" at all, was not encouraged to make comparisons, for in entitling the new collection *Idylls*, Tennyson clearly distinguished it from the "Morte," which had borne the prefatory title "The Epic." The four new poems are all loosely linked by the theme of true and false love. A rejected title for the 1859 idylls underscores their thematic connection: "The True and the False: Four Idylls of the King." The connections are real but at this stage of the poem's evolution one feels them to be more fortuitous than intrinsic. Enid, the true wife who appears false to the suspicious Geraint, contrasts with Guinevere, the false wife who appears true to the unsuspicious Arthur. The harlot Vivien, who deceives and destroys her lover Merlin, contrasts with the virgin Elaine, who destroys herself for love. Tennyson's deletion of "Four" from the provisional title suggests his reluctance to commit himself to further poems in the series, the neutral *Idylls of the King* leaving it to the reader to surmise if more were to come. The four idylls were composed between 1856 and 1859, and in the 1859 edition were entitled "Enid," "Vivien," "Elaine," and "Guinevere." "Enid" was divided into two parts in 1873 and given the final

titles of "The Marriage of Geraint" and "Geraint and Enid" in 1886. (See Ricks, *Poems*, p. 1525.)

26. Buckley, *Tennyson*, pp. 172–173.

27. Hallam's review of *Poems, Chiefly Lyrical* (1830) appeared in the *Englishman's Magazine* of August 1831, when he was not yet twenty, and is reprinted in Jump, *Tennyson*, pp. 34–49.

28. For the quotation from Donald Smalley, see "A New Look at Tennyson—and Especially the *Idylls*," *Journal of English and Germanic Philology*, 51 (1962), 356. For Tennyson's influence on the Symbolists, see Marjorie Bowden, *Tennyson in France* (Manchester, Eng., Manchester University Press, 1930), pp. 56–57, 100–101, 112, 134; Valerie Pitt, *Tennyson Laureate* (London, Barrie and Rockliff, 1962), p. 6; H. M. McLuhan, "Tennyson and Picturesque Poetry," reprinted in Killham, *Critical Essays*, pp. 67–70. Mallarmé's translation of "Mariana" appeared in the October 18, 1874, issue of *La Dernière Mode*, the review which he founded. See also his obituary appreciation of Tennyson entitled "Tennyson vu d'ici," *The National Observer*, October 24, 1892, pp. 611–612. For Baudelaire's borrowing from "The Lotos-Eeaters," see *Le Voyage*, VII, strophes 5 and 6. For Poe's praise of Tennyson, see "The Poetic Principle," *The Complete Works of Edgar Allan Poe*, vol. XIV, ed. James A. Harrison (New York, Fred De Fou, 1902), p. 289.

29. For further speculation on the classical idyll in relation to Tennyson and modern poetry, see H. M. McLuhan's lively "Introduction" to *Alfred Lord Tennyson: Selected Poetry* (New York, Rinehart, 1956), pp. xiv–xv, xxi. See also J. M. Gray, "A Study in Idyl: Tennyson's 'The Coming of Arthur,' " *Renaissance and Modern Studies*, 14 (1970), 111–150.

30. In addition to reversing the order of certain tales, Tennyson transposes characters and settings in others. In Malory's version of "Lancelot and Elaine," as the barge bearing the dead Elaine appears, "by fortune King Arthur and Queen Guenever were speaking together at a window" (bk. XVIII, ch. 20). Tennyson retains Malory's setting but replaces the narratively irrelevant Arthur with Lancelot, who pays tribute to Guinevere at the moment Elaine's barge passes by. The shift is slight but crucial, for the scene now symbolizes the larger narrative of which it is a part: Lancelot at the apex of a tragic triangle, torn between his dying love for the guilty Guinevere and his innocent love for the dead Elaine.

31. The phrase is from an unpublished essay by Pearl Chesler

on "Men and Women in the *Idylls of the King.*"

32. See Kathleen Tillotson's discussion of this point in *Studies*, pp. 91, 106–107.

33. Although "Gareth and Lynette" and "Pelleas and Ettarre" are widely separated in the published order of the idylls, Tennyson began work on one immediately after finishing the other, which perhaps accounts for their closeness in theme and characterization. He wrote most of "Pelleas and Ettarre" in the summer of 1869, completed it by September, and turned to "Gareth and Lynette" later that month or very early in October. Unlike "Pelleas and Ettarre," however, "Gareth and Lynette" gave him great difficulty and he did not complete it until 1872, when it was published together with "The Last Tournament" (which had first appeared separately the previous year). The difficulty, one suspects, arose from Tennyson's going back to the bright beginnings of the realm and working in a deliberately light vein, just after completing the somber "Pelleas and Ettarre" and before starting the later, darker idylls of "The Last Tournament" and "Balin and Balan."

The tangled history of the composition and publication of the *Idylls* is unraveled in Sir Charles Tennyson's *Alfred Tennyson*, in his "The Idylls of the King" (*Twentieth Century* 51 [1957], 277–286), and in Kathleen Tillotson's *Studies*, pp. 80–109. Less detailed but more accessible accounts appear in the headnotes to the separate idylls in Ricks's *Poems*. I have collated these and other sources (not always in agreement) in the following list:

Idyll	Date of Composition	Date of Publication
"Morte d'Arthur" (lines 170–440 of "The Passing of Arthur")	1833–1834	1842
"Merlin and Vivien"	1856	1859
"The Marriage of Geraint"	1856	1859
"Geraint and Enid"	1856	1859
"Guinevere"	1857–1858	1859
"Lancelot and Elaine"	1858–1859	1859
"Dedication"	1861	1862
"The Holy Grail"	1868	1869
"The Coming of Arthur"	1869	1869
"Pelleas and Ettarre"	1869	1869
"Gareth and Lynette"	1869–1872	1872

Idyll	Date of Composition	Date of Publication
"The Passing of Arthur"	1869	1869
"The Last Tournament"	1870–1871	1871
"To the Queen"	1872	1873
"Balin and Balan"	1872–1874	1885

From the list it will be seen that, after the initial impetus that produced the "Morte d'Arthur," Tennyson's work on the *Idylls* was concentrated into two periods, roughly a decade apart. The first, from 1856 (or late in 1855) to 1859, resulted in the 1859 *Idylls of the King* (the Geraint idylls, "Merlin and Vivien," "Lancelot and Elaine," and "Guinevere"). The second, from 1868 to 1874, produced all the remaining idylls, with "Balin and Balan" a kind of tailpiece. "The Coming of Arthur," "The Holy Grail," "Pelleas and Ettarre," and "The Passing of Arthur" were published in the 1869 *The Holy Grail and Other Poems.* "Gareth and Lynette" and "The Last Tournament" appeared in the 1872–1873 Imperial Library Edition of Tennyson's *Works,* together with the eight previously published idylls. At this stage Tennyson believed that he required additional idylls "to make Vivien come later into the Poem" (Ricks, *Poems,* p. 1465), and the long-delayed appearance of "Balin and Balan" may have reflected his desire to publish it with an as-yet-unwritten companion, also to precede "Merlin and Vivien." If I am correct, the abandoning of this intention was signaled by Tennyson's publication of "Balin and Balan" in 1885, followed by the division of "Geraint and Enid" into two independently entitled idylls in 1886 (thus completing the "twelve books" mentioned in the "Morte"). In 1888—fifty-five years after its inception—Tennyson published the collected *Idylls* in their final form.

34. Baum, *Tennyson,* p. 213; Ricks, *Tennyson* (New York, Macmillan, 1972), p. 264; Arthur Christopher Benson, *Alfred Tennyson* (1907; reprint ed., New York, Greenwood Press, 1969), p. 198; T. S. Eliot, cited above, p. 5; John Heath-Stubbs, *The Darkling Plain* (London, Eyre and Spottiswoode, 1950), p. xiv.

III · Timescape

1. H. Tennyson, *Memoir,* II, 127.
2. See Frank Kermode, *The Sense of an Ending* (New York, Oxford University Press, 1967), pp. 9–17.

3. Charles Tennyson, *Alfred Tennyson* (London, Macmillan, 1950), pp. 490–491.

4. Gray, "A Study in Idyl," p. 121.

5. John 19:5. The line from the coronation anthem—"The King will follow Christ, and we the King"—is later repeated by Gareth's "follow the Christ, the King" (GL, 116), which in turn alludes to Paul's injunction, "Be ye followers of me, even as I also am of Christ" (I Corinthians 11:1). Gareth's impatient question to Bellicent—"Who should be King save him who makes us free?"—finds its answer in the Gospel's "the truth shall make you free" (John 8:32). And Arthur's skepticism on learning of the knights' vow to seek the Grail—" 'Lo, now,' said Arthur, 'have ye seen a cloud? / What go ye into the wilderness to see?' " (HG, 286–287)—is a virtual paraphrase of Christ's question to the multitude concerning John the Baptist: "What went ye out into the wilderness to see? A reed shaken with the wind?" (Matthew 11:7). Less overt than these allusions, yet still serving to invest Arthur with a Christlike aura, is a probable parallelism between the taking of the vows and the Sermon on the Mount. The knights are "dazed" after Arthur speaks words of "great authority"; after Jesus delivers the sermon, "the people were astonished at his doctrine: for he taught them as one having authority" (Matthew 7:28–29).

6. H. Tennyson, *Memoir*, II, 127.

7. In calculating the chronology of the realm, I am indebted to M. W. Maccallum's *Tennyson's "Idylls of the King" and Arthurian Story from the XVIth Century* (Glasgow, 1894), pp. 423–428. Maccallum is a kind of lesser A. C. Bradley of the *Idylls* and remains one of its most valuable critics.

8. The coronation anthem is a late addition (1873) to "The Coming of Arthur," and the quoted excerpt from "The Passing" did not appear in the original "Morte d'Arthur." The linked passages illustrate how much of the poem's thematic unity was the product of painstaking evolution.

9. The word *sun* occurs with the following frequency: CA, 10; GL, 11; MG, 7; GE, 6; BB, 1; MV, 2; LE, 5; HG, 3; PE, 2; LT, 1; G, 2; PA, 2. The later uses of the word include Guinevere's guilt-ridden dream of standing before a setting sun (G, 75–82); Tristram's recollection of the radiant young Arthur (LT, 660–663); and the simile comparing the face of the dying King, once "like a rising sun," to a "withered moon" (PA, 380–386). For a perceptive analysis of the cycles of day and year in the

Idylls, see Philip L. Elliott, "Imagery and Unity in the *Idylls of the King*," *Furman Studies,* 15 (1968), 23–28.

10. The same image recurs elsewhere in Tennyson's poetry:

Like that strange song I heard Apollo sing,
While Ilion like a mist rose into towers.

("Tithonus," 62–63)

Here me, for I will speak, and build up all
My sorrow with my song, as yonder walls
Rose slowly to a music slowly breathed.

("Oenone," 38–40)

11. H. Tennyson, *Memoir,* II, 133.

12. It has also been ten years since the heathen attacked Astolat, mutilating the servant who later ferries the dead Elaine to Camelot (271–272), and Lancelot's account of "Arthur's glorious wars" against the heathen locates the twelve battles in the same point of time (284ff.). Assuming that the battles consumed Arthur's energies in his first year as king and that the Diamond Tournament was instituted in the second, we are now in the tenth year of the calendar of the reign.

13. The first four idylls, for example, contain half again as many lines as the last four.

IV · Landscape

1. George Santayana, *Interpretations of Poetry and Religion* (New York, Scribners, 1916), pp. 272–273.

2. H. Tennyson, *Memoir,* I, 11, 172.

3. Santayana, *Interpretations,* p. 275.

4. David Palmer, "The Laureate in Lyonnesse," *The Listener,* 77 (1967), 816–817.

5. For a more detailed analysis of this scene, see Lawrence Poston, " 'Pelleas and Ettarre': Tennyson's 'Troilus,' " *Victorian Poetry,* 4 (1966), 201–202.

6. In II Kings 3 Moab rebels against Israel and on the morning of the battle, "the sun shone upon the water, and the Moabites saw the water on the other side as red as blood: And they said, This is blood . . . now therefore, Moab, to the spoil" (22–23).

7. *King Arthur's Laureate: A Study of Tennyson's "Idylls of the King"* (New York, New York University Press, 1971), p. 35.

8. Nearly half of all the uses in the *Idylls* of *fall* as noun and verb are concentrated in the Geraint poems.

9. *Tennyson: Aspects of His Life, Character and Poetry* (Garden City, N.Y., Doubleday, 1962), p. 323. This work is a later edition of the 1923 volume with an additional "Afterword."

10. Only the "Morte d'Arthur" and "Merlin and Vivien" were composed before the Geraint idylls, which were written immediately after Tennyson completed "Merlin and Vivien" in 1856. Both of the earlier poems attained much of their present resonance by virtue of later additions and revisions, unlike the Geraint idylls, which underwent relatively little revision.

11. I am indebted for this point to J. M. Gray's admirable essay, *Tennyson's Doppelgänger: "Balin and Balan,"* Tennyson Society Monographs, no. 3 (Lincoln, Eng., The Tennyson Society, 1971), p. 29n3. These pages on "Balin and Balan" were drafted before I had read Gray's work on the *Idylls,* and it is evident that we have thought along parallel lines. I have only recently discovered that we were both anticipated in our analysis of "Balin and Balan" by a few suggestive phrases in David Rogers' *Tennyson's "Idylls of the King" and Other Poems,* Monarch Notes and Study Guides (New York, Monarch Press, 1965). One does not normally expect great light to be cast from a "crib," but despite its unfortunate format Rogers' book is at times an excellent guide to the symbolism of the poem.

12. Matthew 26:18. The line is repeated in the first and last chapters of Revelation.

13. John 12:23.

14. LT, 125. A few lines earlier Arthur says, "Oft I seem as he / Of whom was written, 'A sound is in his ears' " (115–116). Cf. Job 15:21: "A dreadful sound is in his ears: in prosperity the destroyer shall come upon him."

15. PA, 214. Cf. 341–343, where Bedivere carries the dying King "through the place of tombs," and Matthew 27:33: "They were come unto a place called Golgotha, that is to say, a place of a skull."

16. Cf. Revelation 21:2, 21: "And I John saw the holy city . . . And the twelve gates were twelve pearls; every several gate was of one pearl."

17. Revelation 18:8.

18. The flaming shadows that broaden from Guinevere's feet may also allude to the scene in Malory (bk. XX, ch. 7) in which Arthur condemns her to be burned at the stake for infidelity.

19. Ricks, *Poems,* p. 1745; H. Tennyson, *Memoir,* II, 132.

20. Revelation 16:19–21. Tennyson himself points out the parallelism between the biblical text and his own in a note cited in Ricks, *Poems,* p. 1745.

21. GL, 21–22; HG, 237–240. For a perceptive analysis of the changed perspective through which we view Arthur, see Francis Patrick Devlin, "Tennyson's Use of Landscape Imagery" (Ph.D. diss., Indiana University, 1968), pp. 272–273.

V • *Character and Symbol*

1. *A General Introduction to Psychoanalysis,* trans. Joan Riviere (Garden City, N.Y., Garden City Publishing Co., 1943), p. 204.

2. *Essays and Introductions* (New York, Macmillan, 1961), p. 159.

3. H. Tennyson, *Memoir,* I, 320.

4. Ibid., II, 90.

5. *Sartor Resartus,* ed. Charles F. Harrold (New York, Odyssey Press, 1937), p. 223.

6. Jump, *Tennyson,* p. 48.

7. See Freud, *General Introduction,* pp. 191–194, and Frye, *Anatomy of Criticism,* pp. 186–187.

8. "Tennyson," *Prose and Poetry* (London, Jonathan Cape, 1947), p. 79.

9. The most marked resemblance is that between Gareth's second adversary, "Huge on a huge red horse" (1000) and armed with a mighty sword, and the second Horseman of the Apocalypse: "And there went out another horse that was red: and power was given to him that sat thereon to take peace from the earth . . . and there was given unto him a great sword" (Revelation 6:4). For further similarities between the sets of horsemen, see W. David Shaw, "Gareth's Four Antagonists: A Biblical Source," *Victorian Newsletter,* 34 (1968), 34–35.

10. See bk. IV, ch. 20–23.

11. Cf. Percivale's description of her:

A holy maid; though never maiden glowed,
But that was in her earlier maidenhood,
With such a fervent flame of human love,
Which being rudely blunted, glanced and shot
Only to holy things . . .   (HG, 72–76)

The "fervent flame of human love" may also be detected in the Nun's description of the long beam on which the Grail enters her cell, quivering rose-red as if alive (117–123). She weaves a sword-belt for Galahad of her own hair, interlacing in its design crimson and silver threads emblematic of her passion and purity and reminiscent of the scarlet and pearl sleeve that Elaine presents to Lancelot.

12. Cf. her similar misapprehension of Balin's motives for trampling upon the Queen's crest, which is emblazoned on his shield:

> This fellow hath wrought some foulness with his Queen:
> Else never had he borne her crown, nor raved
> And thus foamed over at a rival name.
>
> (556–558)

Delusion, however, is as much the property of the good characters in the *Idylls* as of the evil. The dying Balan assures his twin, "Pure as our own true Mother is our Queen" (606).

13. Cited in Nicolson, *Tennyson*, 1923 ed., p. 224.

14. "Microscope," *Complete Works*, XVI, 409.

15. Bk. IV, ch. 1. For Tennyson's chief source, the Vulgate *Merlin*, see Ricks, *Poems*, pp. 1594–1595.

16. John 4:18. Later in the same speech Vivien recalls Mark's mocking reference to Arthur's purity: "There is no being pure, / My cherub; saith not Holy Writ the same?" (51–52). Cf. Proverbs 20:9: "Who can say, I have made my heart clean, I am pure from my sin?" At the close of "Balin and Balan" Vivien's exclamation over the dying brothers—"I better prize / The living dog than the dead lion: away! / I cannot brook to gaze upon the dead" (573–575)—paraphrases the line in Ecclesiastes, "For a living dog is better than a dead lion" (9:4). When Merlin repulses her with the word *harlot*, she breaks into tears and accuses him of stabbing her "through the heart's affections to the heart! / Seethed like the kid in its own mother's milk!" (MV, 866–867). Again, she alludes to the Bible to subvert its intention and further her own. Cf. Exodus 34:26—"Thou shalt not seethe a kid in his mother's milk"—and Deut. 14:21, where the verse is repeated.

17. Hosea 8:7. See also Stopford A. Brooke, *Tennyson: His Art and Relation to Modern Life* (London, Isbister, 1894), pp. 290–291.

18. Tennyson employs still another biblical analogue—Samson and Delilah—for the scene in which Vivien, drawing "the vast and shaggy mantle" of Merlin's beard across her breast, exclaims, "Lo, I clothe myself with wisdom" (253–255). Gordon Haight suggests that Tennyson's characterization of Vivien as a serpent was influenced by an illustration he saw in Southey's edition of *The Byrth, Lyf, and Actes of Kyng Arthur* (1817). The story of Merlin and Vivien opens with "a grotesque ornamental capital S formed by an enormous serpent . . . winding itself about the ankle and across the knees of a naked man." *Studies in Philology,* 44 (1947), 552.

19. The wavering movement of Tristram's mind is perfectly caught in the following lines:

Before him fled the face of Queen Isolt
With ruby-circled neck, but evermore
Past, as a rustle or twitter in the wood
Made dull his inner, keen his outer eye
For all that walked, or crept, or perched, or flew.
Anon the face, as, when a gust hath blown,
Unruffling waters re-collect the shape
Of one that in them sees himself, returned;
But at the slot or fewmets of a deer,
Or even a fallen feather, vanished again.

(363–372)

20. Cf. Matthew 7:16: "Ye shall know them by their fruits. Do men gather grapes of thorns, or figs of thistles?"

21. Comparison with Malory here cannot be invidious, for Malory's closing scenes cannot be surpassed: "And therefore, lady, sithen ye have taken to perfection, I must needs take me to perfection . . . For my sorrow was not, nor is not, for any rejoicing of sin, but my sorrow may never have end." (Bk. XXI, chs. 9 and 11.)

22. See ll. 1000–1011 for her "Song of Love and Death." The funeral barge is in fact a kind of marriage chamber; Elaine has her deathbed decked "like the Queen's / . . . and me also like the Queen," and she drapes over herself the embroidered case she has stripped from Lancelot's "naked shield" (1110–1112, 1141–1142, 972).

23. The distinction is nicely drawn when we first see them together in Guinevere's garden. Pearl Chesler points out that

Guinevere "has the 'morning on her face,' while he is 'all in shadow.' She has the light with her because she has an undivided will; no part of her is hidden from herself." (Unpublished essay, "Men and Women in *Idylls of the King*.")

24. Cf. Daniel 3:19: "Then was Nebuchadnezzär full of fury, . . . and commanded that they should heat the furnace one seven times more than it was wont to be heated."

25. H. Tennyson, *Memoir*, II, 129. Cf. *Materials*, III, 201, where Hallam writes that "A. T. thought that perhaps he had not made the historical reality of the King sufficiently clear."

26. The long struggle that finally brings Guinevere to Almesbury reaches all the way back to "Lancelot and Elaine," where she tells Lancelot that she has "done despite and wrong" to one nobler than himself (1202). Tennyson further prepares for her repentance at the grimly inauspicious start of the Grail quest, when she rides alongside Lancelot and shrieks aloud, "This madness has come on us for our sins" (HG, 357).

27. Cf. Arthur's first words after the trumpet sounds: "Yet think not that I come to urge thy crimes," "I, whose vast pity almost makes me die" (529, 531). But Arthur *has* just urged her crimes, and while he doubtless feels vast pity, and Tennyson wants us to perceive its Christlike quality, Arthur's first-person proclamation vitiates Tennyson's intention.

28. Swinburne, "Microscope," *Complete Works*, XVI, 404–405. The essay makes the classic case against what Swinburne liked to call the "Morte d'Albert, or Idylls of the Prince Consort": "Mr. Tennyson has lowered the note and deformed the outline of the Arthurian story, by reducing Arthur to the level of a wittol, Guinevere to the level of a woman of intrigue, and Launcelot to the level of a 'co-respondent.' Treated as he treated it, the story is rather a case for the divorce-court than for poetry." See also Jump, *Tennyson*, p. 339.

29. Bk. XX, ch. 9.

VI · *Symbol and Story*

1. This significance is evident enough in Merlin's fears that Arthur's high purpose will be "broken by the worm" (MV, 194) and in the love song entitled "A Worm within the Rose" in "Pelleas and Ettarre."

2. HG, 481–483; PE, 597. Cf. Matthew 26:18.

3. In the course of the seduction scene Vivien reminds Merlin

that she had once "bathed [his] feet before her own" (282).
This gesture of reverence and charity on the part of the
Antichrist of the *Idylls* mockingly alludes to the passage in
John in which Jesus washes the feet of the disciples (13:5–16).
Cf. Luke 7:37–38, in which a sinner bathes Jesus' feet "with tears,
and did wipe them with the hairs of her head, and kissed
his feet."

4. Clyde Ryals notes a further parallelism between the two
queens, both of whom look upon "love as an escape—Guinevere
from almost absolute goodness, Isolt from almost absolute evil."
From the Great Deep, p. 129.

5. Cf. Tennyson's very different use of Percivale as narrator
of "The Holy Grail." Percivale's dramatic monologue constitutes
virtually all of the idyll, and his voice is clearly differentiated by
quotation marks from that of the omniscient narrator. Bedivere
functions far more problematically in "The Passing." He is
introduced in a brief opening paragraph that serves to frame
the narrative:

That story which the bold Sir Bedivere,
First made and latest left of all the knights,
Told, when the man was no more than a voice
In the white winter of his age, to those
With whom he dwelt, new faces, other minds.

But the frame (which is in fact a sentence fragment) is quickly
forgotten, and the balance of the idyll is recounted not by
Bedivere but by the omniscient narrator.

6. See, for example, CA, 94; GL, 1392–1394; GE, 161; PE, 482;
LT, 226.

7. Cf. a comparable passage in "The Coming of Arthur" in
which Bellicent urges Leodogran

     to give this King thine only child,
Guinevere: so great bards of him will sing
Hereafter . . .

                       (412–414)

8. The most complex interweaving of song and narrative occurs
in "Guinevere." As the repentant Queen rides to Almesbury, she
laments to herself, "Too late, too late!" (130). The reiterated
phrase then appears in the refrain—"Too late, too late! ye cannot
enter now"—of the novice's song of repentance (166–177), which

in turn alludes to the parable of the wise and foolish virgins.
At one point the novice sings, "O let us in, though late, to kiss
his feet!"—a line which Guinevere enacts a few lines later at the
feet of Arthur, the "bridegroom [who] will relent." Finally the
refrain rejoins the narrative after Arthur's departure, when, "still
hoping, fearing," Guinevere asks herself, "Is it yet too late?" (685).
One observes the same close connection of song to story in
"The Marriage of Geraint." Yniol repeats verbatim in the narrative
the line—"Our hoard is little, but our hearts are great"—that
Enid has sung moments earlier in her refrain, "Turn, Fortune,
Turn Thy Wheel" (352, 374). The song foretells the reversal in
Enid's fortune from penury to marriage with Geraint, back to
penury again when he abuses her, and finally to prosperous
reconciliation.

Bibliography

The Bibliography lists all works cited in the text, with the exception of certain unpublished materials that have been identified in the footnotes. I have also included several works that have significantly shaped my own understanding of Tennyson although they have not been quoted. Critical or biographical studies that the reader might find especially illuminating have been indicated by an asterisk.

Abbott, C. C., ed. *The Correspondence of Gerard Manley Hopkins and Richard Watson Dixon.* London, Oxford University Press, 1935.

Alford, Henry. "The *Idylls of the King,*" *Contemporary Review,* 13 (1870), 104–125.

Auden, W. H., ed. *A Selection from the Poems of Alfred, Lord Tennyson.* Garden City, N.Y., Doubleday, Doran & Co., 1944.

Bagehot, Walter. "Wordsworth, Tennyson, and Browning; or Pure, Ornate and Grotesque Art in English Poetry," *Literary Studies.* 1864. Reprint: London, Dent, 1950.

Baker, Arthur E. *A Concordance to the Poetical and Dramatic Works of Alfred, Lord Tennyson.* London, Kegan Paul, Trench, Trübner, 1914.

Baum, Paull F. *Tennyson Sixty Years After.* Chapel Hill, N.C., University of North Carolina Press, 1948.

Benson, Arthur C. *Alfred Tennyson.* 1907. Reprint: New York. Greenwood Press, 1969.

Berry, Francis. "The Voice of Tennyson," *Poetry and the Physical Voice*. London, Routledge & Kegan Paul, 1962.

Boas, Frederick S. "*Idylls of the King* in 1921," *Nineteenth Century and After*, 40 (November 1921), 819–830.

Bowden, Marjorie. "Tennyson and the Symbolist Movement," *Tennyson in France*. Manchester, Eng., University of Manchester Press, 1930.

Bradley, A. C. "The Long Poem in the Age of Wordsworth," *Oxford Lectures on Poetry*. London, Macmillan, 1909.

Brashear, William R. *The Living Will: A Study of Tennyson and Nineteenth-Century Subjectivism*. The Hague, Mouton, 1969.

Brooke, Stopford A. *Tennyson: His Art and Relation to Modern Life*. London, Isbister, 1894.

Brooks, Cleanth. "The Motivation of Tennyson's Weeper," *The Well-Wrought Urn: Studies in the Structure of Poetry*. New York, Harcourt, Brace and Co., 1947.

*Buckley, Jerome H. "The City Built to Music," *Tennyson: The Growth of a Poet*. Cambridge, Mass., Harvard University Press, 1960.

———*The Victorian Temper*. Cambridge, Mass., Harvard University Press, 1951.

Burchell, S. C. "Tennyson's 'Allegory in the Distance,' " *PMLA*, 68 (1953), 418–424.

Carlyle, Thomas. *Sartor Resartus*, ed. Charles F. Harrold. New York, Odyssey Press, 1937.

*Carr, Arthur J. "Tennyson as a Modern Poet," *Critical Essays on the Poetry of Tennyson*, ed. John Killham. London, Routledge & Kegan Paul, 1960.

Clark, Kenneth. *Landscape into Art*. New York, Scribners, 1950.

Cross, Tom P. "Alfred Tennyson as a Celticist," *Modern Philology*, 18 (1921), 485–492.

Danzig, Allan. "The Contraries: A Central Concept in Tennyson's Poetry," *PMLA*, 77 (1962), 577–585.

DeMott, Benjamin. "The Voice of Lotos-Land," *Hells and Benefits*. New York, Basic Books, 1962.

Devlin, Francis Patrick. "Tennyson's Use of Landscape Imagery." Ph.D. diss., Indiana University, 1968.

Dodsworth, Martin. "Patterns of Morbidity: Repetition in Tennyson's Poetry," *The Major Victorian Poets: Reconsiderations*, ed. Isobel Armstrong. London, Routledge & Kegan Paul, 1969.

*Eggers, J. Philip. *King Arthur's Laureate: A Study of Tennyson's Idylls of the King.* New York, New York University Press, 1971.

Eliot, T. S. *The Complete Poems and Plays, 1909–1950.* New York, Harcourt, Brace & World, 1952.

*——"In Memoriam," *Selected Essays,* 3rd ed. London, Faber and Faber, 1951.

Elliott, Philip L. "Imagery and Unity in the *Idylls of the King,*" *Furman Studies,* 15 (1968), 22–28.

*Engelberg, Edward. "The Beast Image in Tennyson's *Idylls of the King,*" *ELH,* 22 (1955), 287–292.

Freud, Sigmund. *Character and Culture,* ed. Philip Rieff. New York, Collier Books, 1963.

——*A General Introduction to Psychoanalysis,* trans. Joan Riviere, preface by Ernest Jones and G. Stanley Hall. Garden City, N.Y., Garden City Publishing Co., 1943.

Frye, Northrop. *Anatomy of Criticism: Four Essays.* Princeton, N.J., Princeton University Press, 1957.

*Gray, J. M. "A Study in Idyl: Tennyson's 'The Coming of Arthur,'" *Renaissance and Modern Studies,* 14 (1970), 111–150.

——*Tennyson's Doppelgänger: "Balin and Balan."* Tennyson Society Monographs, no. 3. Lincoln, Eng., The Tennyson Society, 1971.

Haight, Gordon S. "Tennyson's Merlin," *Studies in Philology,* 44 (1947), 549–566.

*Hallam, Arthur H. "On Some of the Characteristics of Modern Poetry, and on the Lyrical Poems of Alfred Tennyson," *Englishmen's Magazine,* August 1831, pp. 616–628. Reprinted in *Tennyson: The Critical Heritage,* ed. John D. Jump, London, Routledge & Kegan Paul, 1967.

Hartman, Joan E. "The Manuscripts of Tennyson's 'Gareth and Lynette,'" *Harvard Library Bulletin,* 13 (1959), 239–264.

Heath-Stubbs, John. *The Darkling Plain.* London, Eyre & Spottiswoode, 1950.

Hone, Joseph. *W. B. Yeats, 1865–1939.* London, Macmillan, 1942.

Hough, Graham, ed. *George Meredith: Selected Poems.* London, Oxford University Press, 1962.

Johnson, E. D. H. "Alfred, Lord Tennyson," *The Victorian Poets: A Guide to Research,* ed. Frederick E. Faverty, 2nd ed. Cambridge, Mass., Harvard University Press, 1968.

*————"Tennyson," *The Alien Vision of Victorian Poetry.*
Princeton, N.J., Princeton University Press, 1952.

Jones, Richard. *The Growth of the Idylls of the King.* Philadelphia,
J. B. Lippincott, 1895.

Joseph, Gerhard. *Tennysonian Love: The Strange Diagonal.*
Minneapolis, University of Minnesota Press, 1969.

Jump, John D., ed. *Tennyson: The Critical Heritage.* London,
Routledge & Kegan Paul, 1967.

Kaplan, Fred. "Woven Paces and Waving Hands: Tennyson's
Merlin as Fallen Artist," *Victorian Poetry*, 7 (1969), 285–298.

Kenner, Hugh, ed. *T. S. Eliot: A Collection of Critical Essays.*
Englewod Cliffs, N.J., Prentice-Hall, 1962.

Kermode, Frank. *The Sense of an Ending: Studies in the Theory
of Fiction.* New York, Oxford University Press, 1967.

Killham, John, ed. *Critical Essays on the Poetry of Tennyson.*
London, Routledge & Kegan Paul, 1960.

Kissane, James D. *Alfred Tennyson.* New York, Twayne, 1970.

————"Tennyson: The Passion of the Past and the Curse of
Time," *ELH*, 32 (1965), 85–109.

Knowles, James T. "Tennyson's Arthurian Poem," *Tennyson and
His Friends*, ed. Hallam, Lord Tennyson. London,
Macmillan, 1911.

Leavis, F. R. *New Bearings in English Poetry*, 2nd ed. London,
Chatto & Windus, 1950.

Littledale, Harold. *Essays on Lord Tennyson's Idylls of the King*,
2nd ed. London, Macmillan, 1912.

Litzinger, Boyd. "The Structure of Tennyson's 'Last
Tournament,'" *Victorian Poetry*, 1 (1963), 53–60.

Lucas, F. L. *Ten Victorian Poets.* Cambridge, Cambridge
University Press, 1940.

Macaulay, G. C., ed. *The Holy Grail.* London, Macmillan, 1893.

MacCallum, Mungo W. *Tennyson's "Idylls of the King" and
Arthurian Story from the Sixteenth Century.* Glasgow,
Maclehouse & Sons, 1894.

McLuhan, Herbert Marshall. "The Aesthetic Moment in
Landscape Poetry," *English Institute Essays; 1951*, ed. Alan S.
Downer. New York, Columbia University Press, 1952.

————"Introduction," *Alfred Lord Tennyson: Selected Poetry.*
New York, Holt, Rinehart, & Winston, 1956.

*————"Tennyson and Picturesque Poetry," *Critical Essays on
the Poetry of Tennyson*, ed. John Killham. London,
Routledge & Kegan Paul, 1960.

Mallarmé, Stéphane. "Tennyson vu d'ici," *The National Observer*, October 24, 1892, pp. 611–612.

Malory, Sir Thomas. *Le Morte d'Arthur*, 2 vols. Everyman's Library. London, Dent, 1906.

Meynell, Alice. "Tennyson," *Alice Meynell: Poetry and Prose*, intro. by V. Sackville-West. London, Jonathan Cape, 1947.

Miller, Betty. "Tennyson and the Sinful Queen," *Twentieth Century*, 158 (1955), 355–363.

Nicolson, Harold. *Tennyson: Aspects of His Life, Character, and Poetry*. London, Constable and Constable, 1923. Reprint. Garden City, N.Y., Doubleday, 1962. (The reprint contains "Afterword, 1960.")

Paden, W. D. *Tennyson in Egypt: A Study of the Imagery in His Earlier Work*. Lawrence, Kans., University of Kansas Press, 1942.

Pallen, Condé Benoist. *The Meaning of the "Idylls of the King": An Essay in Interpretation*. New York, American Book Co., 1904.

Palmer, David. "The Laureate in Lyonnesse," *The Listener*, 77 (1967), 815–817.

Peckham, Morse. *Victorian Revolutionaries: Speculations on Some Heroes of a Culture Crisis*. New York, Braziller, 1970. (Chapter 1 is on Tennyson.)

*Pitt, Valerie. *Tennyson Laureate*. London, Barrie & Rockliff, 1962.

Poe, Edgar Allan. "The Poetic Principle," *The Complete Works of Edgar Allan Poe*, vol. XIV, ed. James A. Harrison. New York, Fred De Fou, 1902.

Poston, Lawrence III. "The Argument of the Geraint-Enid Books in *Idylls of the King*," *Victorian Poetry*, 2 (1964), 269–275.

———" 'Pelleas and Ettarre': Tennyson's 'Troilus,' " *Victorian Poetry*, 4 (1966), 199–204.

———"The Two Provinces of Tennyson's *Idylls*," *Criticism*, 9 (1967), 372–382.

*Priestley, F. E. L. "*Idylls of the King*—A Fresh View," *Critical Essays on the Poetry of Tennyson*, ed. John Killham. London, Routledge & Kegan Paul, 1960.

Reed, John R. *Perception and Design in Tennyson's "Idylls of the King."* Athens, Ohio, Ohio Universtiy Press, 1969.

*Ricks, Christopher. *Tennyson*. New York, Macmillan, 1972.

———"The Tennyson Manuscripts," *Times Literary Supplement*, August 21, 1969, pp. 918–922.

————"Tennyson's Methods of Composition," *Proceedings of the British Academy*, 52 (1966), 209–230.

Robb, Kenneth Alan. "The Structure of Tennyson's *Idylls of the King*." Ph.D. diss., University of Wisconsin, 1966.

Robinson, Edna M. *Tennyson's Use of the Bible*. 1917. Reprint. New York, Gordian Press, 1968.

Rogers, David. *Tennyson's Idylls of the King and Other Poems*. New York, Monarch Press, 1965.

Rosenberg, John D. "The Two Kingdoms of *In Memoriam*," *Journal of English and Germanic Philology*, 58 (1959), 228–240.

Ryals, Clyde de L. *From the Great Deep: Essays on "Idylls of the King."* Athens, Ohio, Ohio University Press, 1967.

Santayana, George. "The Elements and Function of Poetry," *Interpretations of Poetry and Religion*. New York, Harper, 1957.

Shannon, Edgar F., Jr., "The Proofs of 'Gareth and Lynette' in the Widener Collection," *Papers of the Bibliographical Society of America*, 41 (1947), 321–340.

Shaw, W. David. "Gareth's Four Antagonists: A Biblical Source," *Victorian Newsletter*, 34 (1968), 34–35.

————"*Idylls of the King*: A Dialectical Reading," *Victorian Poetry*, 7 (1969), 175–190.

Slater, Joseph, ed. *The Correspondence of Emerson and Carlyle*. New York, Columbia University Press, 1964.

Smalley, Donald. "A New Look at Tennyson—and Especially the *Idylls*," *Journal of English and Germanic Philology*, 61 (1962), 349–357.

Smith, Elton E. *The Two Voices: A Tennyson Study*. Lincoln, Neb., University of Nebraska Press, 1964.

Solomon, Stanley J. "Tennyson's Paradoxical King," *Victorian Poetry*, 1 (1963), 258–271.

Swinburne, Algernon Charles. "Under the Microscope," *The Complete Works of Algernon Charles Swinburne*, Bonchurch Edition, vol. XVI, ed. Edmund Gosse and Thomas James Wise. London, Heinemann, 1925–1926.

*Tennyson, Alfred, Lord. *The Poems of Tennyson*, ed. Christopher Ricks. London, Longmans, 1969. (The standard text, with indispensable annotation.)

————*The Poetic and Dramatic Works of Alfred, Lord Tennyson*, ed. W. J. Rolfe. Boston and New York, Houghton Mifflin, 1898.

————*The Works of Alfred, Lord Tennyson*, Eversley Edition, 9 vols., annotated by Alfred, Lord Tennyson, ed. Hallam, Lord Tennyson. London, Macmillan, 1907–1908.

*Tennyson, Charles. *Alfred Tennyson.* London, Macmillan, 1950.

————"The *Idylls of the King*," *Twentieth Century*, 161 (1957), 277–286.

————"Some MSS. of the *Idylls of the King* and a Note on Tennyson as a Narrative Poet," *Six Tennyson Essays.* London, Cassell & Co., 1954.

Tennyson, Charles, and Christine Fall. *Alfred Tennyson: An Annotated Bibliography.* Athens, Ga., University of Georgia Press, 1967.

*Tennyson, Hallam. *Alfred Lord Tennyson: A Memoir*, 2 vols. London, Macmillan, 1897.

————*Materials for a Life of A. T.*, 4 vols. Privately printed, 1895.

————*Tennyson and His Friends.* London, Macmillan, 1911.

*Tillotson, Kathleen. "Tennyson's Serial Poem," *Mid-Victorian Studies*, by Geoffrey and Kathleen Tillotson. London, University of London, Athlone Press, 1965.

Wilkenfeld, R. B. "Tennyson's Camelot: The Kingdom of Folly," *University of Toronto Quarterly*, 37 (1968), 281–294.

Wimsatt, W. K. "Prufrock and Maud: From Plot to Symbol," *Hateful Contraries: Studies in Literature and Criticism.* Lexington, Ky., University of Kentucky Press, 1965.

Yeats, William Butler. *The Letters of W. B. Yeats*, ed. Allan Wade. London, Rupert Hart-Davis, 1954.

————"The Symbolism of Poetry," *Essays and Interpretations.* New York, Macmillan, 1961.

Young, G. M. "The Age of Tennyson," *Critical Essays on the Poetry of Tennyson*, ed. John Killham. London, Routledge & Kegan Paul, 1960.

Index

Except under their main entries, individual idylls are abbreviated according to the Note on Citations on page xi.

175